The Compleat Dean
A Guide to Academic Leadership in an Age of Uncertainty

(compleat: having all necessary or desired elements or skills; quintessential)

"The Compleat Dean" is compiled from answers to 113 questions covering all aspects of being a Vice Chancellor of Health/Dean of a School of Medicine in the United States. The questionnaire was completed by more than half of the 61 individuals who were Vice Chancellors/Deans of a School of Medicine in 2014, and had been in that position for 5 or more years. In sum, the following text represents more than 350 years of contemporary decanal experience.

RALPH V. CLAYMAN, MD

ISBN: 1537377132
ISBN-13: 978-1537377131

DEDICATION

To Carol, without whom there would have been no dean's experience in my life and with whom everything has been possible.
To all Vice Chancellors of Health/Deans of Schools of Medicine who have taken on the responsibility of creating the physicians who will be ministering to the healthcare needs of each of us.

CONTENTS

ACKNOWLEDGMENTS

There would be no book were it not for the willing donation of time and expertise of so many of my colleagues across the United States. In this capacity I have merely served to compile their thoughts, advice, and experiences into a comprehensive text. I need to also thank Ms. Judith Bronson and Ms. Ceileigh Mangalam who helped with the editing of the text. I am also indebted to Ms. Rebecca Brusuelas and Mr. Terry Belmont who sustained me throughout my time as dean and subsequently took the time to carefully read and comment on the contents of this book. However in the final analysis this book would have, like so many unimplemented strategic plans, remained unpublished upon the shelf were it not for Ms. Jenny Tom who in short order was able to take a rough draft and wend it through the wiles of CreateSpace bringing it to its publishable state. To be sure, she is magic.

1. INTRODUCTION

In today's environment, becoming dean of a school of medicine or vice chancellor of an academic health center is a daunting task given current challenges in healthcare, educational models, research funding, and the need for community engagement. Navigating these difficult waters is a challenging journey that for the vast majority ends well shy of a five year term. Having personally served a 5 year term as dean, it was apparent to me how few tools I had to help guide me on this voyage. In looking back there is much I wish I had known prior to setting sail and thus elected to embark on an endeavor to assemble the collective wisdom of a large number of deans/vice chancellors of academic health centers who had successfully held their position for five or more years.

The following text is based on an extensive questionnaire (Appendix I), sent to all medical school/health center deans or vice chancellors in the summer of 2014 who at the time the questionnaire was sent had held their position for 5 or more years. Among the 141 accredited medical schools, only 61 (43%) individuals had reached or exceeded the 5 year mark; 35 (57%) completed and returned the questionnaire. The responding deans were overwhelmingly male (86%) with an average experience of 9.73 years (5.0-23.7 years). As a group, the respondents registered over 350 years of decanal experience.

The book is specifically intended for those individuals who are newly minted deans of a medical school or vice chancellors of health; however, it also is meant for individuals who may aspire to this post as well as current chairs of a department in an academic health center who seek a better understanding of decanal practice. By the same token, this book has general information with regard to leading an academic effort that may be of value to nonmedical deans or department chairs.

2. OVERVIEW

While IQ is most often quoted as an attribute and determinant, it is far and away insufficient in and of itself to foster decanal success; indeed it is the eQ ("e" commonly standing for emotional but in this instance also indicating effectiveness, efficiency, economy, equanimity, and empathy) that makes the difference between a flash of lightning and a long-burning candle; the former, brief albeit spectacular and with all too often destructive consequences versus the latter, a source of light and warmth capable of igniting many other candles along the way much to the enhancement of the institution and its faculty, without diminishing in the least the spark of the leader, from which the other candles were lit.

Decanal career aspirations are rare. Indeed, clear plans to become dean were largely absent (i.e. 90%) among the respondents. However, the leadership abilities and interest of this group were solidly evident as they commonly had experiences as Chairs of Departments as well as other leadership positions within the School of Medicine, the practice plan, and/or the hospital. While some deans in their predecanal years took several day or 1-2 week leadership courses[1], rarely did they seek a more advanced degree[2]. However, upon entering the dean's office, nearly half proceeded to partake of the AAMC's two part course for new deans.

---

[1]Association of American Medical Colleges (AAMC) course for Associate Deans or Harvard course for Clinical Chairs

[2] Masters in Business Administration (MBA) – 6%; Masters in Administrative Medicine – 6%

In an effort to identify the **primary characteristics common** to this group, each respondent was asked to describe themselves in one word. Two traits were most commonly cited: _perseverance_ (e.g. persistent, resilient, obsessed, workaholic, focused/determined, mission oriented, meticulous, responsible, solutions expert) and a _nurturing personality_ (altruistic, optimistic, collaborative, supportive, and coach). The third trait was creativity (e.g., creative and innovative). Infrequently mentioned traits/abilities were honest, transparent, passionate, practical, fair, patient, thriving, learning, and thoughtful. In sum, the most durable deans are those able to nurture their faculty and students while simultaneously being relentlessly focused in their pursuit of fulfilling their school's mission; not surprisingly in these challenging times, creativity followed closely on the heels of the first two characteristics.

Regardless of background, there were many factors for which the new incumbent deans were **unprepared**. The most common "awakening" was the _insular nature of chairs_ and other stakeholders who either are incapable or unwilling to look beyond the needs of their departments in order to embrace the change necessary to benefit the common good of the institution through cultural development and strategic planning/implementation. Similarly the amount of time the deans needed to spend with external stakeholders (legislators, alumni, donors, payers, and business leaders) as well as time spent with the media and affiliate hospital leadership was unanticipated. As one dean noted: "This is a long haul, a marathon – not a sprint." You need to pace yourself. Other cited areas of "surprise" included: the scope and magnitude of the Liaison Committee on Medical Education (LCME) accreditation process, the weakness of advancement (i.e. fundraising) in the medical school, legal issues, politics (both internal and external), and the challenges of a byzantine bureaucracy further complicated by the complexities of modern day electronic record keeping.

On a different note, there were no **earth-shattering epiphanies**. Rather, the responding deans cited the clear realization of how important it was to have the _right people in the right positions_. The most important people were those in the dean's office; this is the team that "has your back"; as such, these individuals must be capable, accountable, and committed. It is essential to take the time to know each member of the team that one has inherited, and then carefully, but assuredly, cull the pleasant but incompetent. Failing to take this bold, and at times unpopular step, will force one to wade into a molasses pit of micromanagement. As one dean noted: "On a good day, I make only half the people mad at me."

In the same vein, the chairs present their own separate challenge as many are resistant to change and the spark for greatness has long since been extinguished; this situation is most common among those chairs who have "been there and seen it all", short in productivity, and impenetrably cocooned within an ongoing state of denial/entitlement. Don't be taken aback when you are told that they expect to "outlast" you and hence see no reason to support any change that you may propose.

So if you weather the initial challenges and remain in the dean's office for a full 5 year term, what **accomplishments** will you come to view as your greatest source of satisfaction? First and foremost is the realization of culture change. Close seconds are recruitment of the right people, solvency, and alterations in the educational curriculum, and the addition of new buildings/facilities to the campus.

The **cultural transformation** of the School of Medicine, medical center, and physician practice plan from multiple separate entities each with their own self-directed goals into a tightly knit entity with an associated air of trust, credibility, metric-based compensation, and "can-do" environment is by far the one most cited element necessary for success. This, coupled with **hiring the right people**, becomes the two key drivers for every success that follows: educational reform, solvency, philanthropy, clinical excellence, and research empowerment. Of note, branding, diversity, strategic planning and community engagement were rarely cited by the responding deans even though each entails a significant investment of time and effort. Instead of an end in and of themselves, they are viewed as the means to potentially effect, the ultimate goal, that of "culture change".

Not surprisingly, the answer to questions regarding the **primary path and biggest obstacle to change** were identical: _people_. These replies took several forms:

a.) perils of expedient hiring (e.g. hiring from within due to time/cost constraints, shorting a search due to an overwhelming push to fill a position, etc.)

b.) failing to act on one's gut impression to not hire an individual

c.) being led by consensus into hiring the wrong person despite your own misgivings

d.) slowness to remove ineffective or self-serving chairs or senior leadership. (The importance of a well-defined timeline to accomplishment and associated metrics were noted to be key elements in empowering the dean to move forward with upper level replacements in a manner that would be perceived as fair and transparent.)

e.) in-depth vetting of candidates (see Chapter 9 on "Hiring and Negotiation" under the section "Vetting the Final Candidate").

Other obstacles to successful change, albeit much less commonly mentioned, had to do with lines and means of communication, development of hospital affiliations, the importance of clearly defining objectives (i.e. what would success look like), creating mutually acceptable timelines to achieve specific goals, the financial perils of expanding a research program too quickly (N.B.: see Chapter 15 "Research: sustainability"), and challenges with integrating the electronic medical record.

3. PROLOG: SIGNING ON (YOUR PACKAGE AND WHAT IT SHOULD INCLUDE)

There are **two ways** to come into the dean's office: as part of a planned succession or as the final act in resolution of a crisis. The former allows for a normal interview process and you as the candidate have time to prepare; indeed, you have elected to be interviewed and presumably this is a post you are seeking. The latter is more like being caught in the middle of a downpour; the leadership is looking for an umbrella and has internally identified you. But like an umbrella you are only being offered the job during the rainstorm and there are no promises of any employ beyond the present deluge; hence you have been saddled with the moniker "interim".

If you are part of a **planned succession**, you have time to prepare. Here are some helpful suggestions:

- Arrive on campus 2-4 weeks BEFORE you are slated to begin your tenure as dean. You should have already done your homework and focused on learning as much as possible about the position.
- Create your own campus personnel guide with names, titles, contacts, background (i.e. years at present institution, prior graduate and undergraduate education) and photographs of all internal stakeholders (i.e. university, School of Medicine and hospital leadership as well as foundation/board members) and external stakeholders (e.g. politicians, affiliate hospital CEO's, community supporters/donors).
- Interview each of the people in your "campus personnel guide" (vide supra) and seek to understand what they consider current successes (best programs in the school or best people in the

school), current problems (biggest challenge in the school), anticipated problems (if you could change one thing in the school, what would it be), and any other suggestions. Alternatively you can use a *"stop, start, continue"* mode of questioning (i.e. what is the School of Medicine doing that it should *stop*? What is the School of Medicine not doing that it should *start*? What is the School of Medicine doing that it should *continue*?). In each of these conversations you should be in receiver-on/transmitter-off mode, listening intently and taking notes; within the replies lurks a clear depiction of the challenges you are facing and a vivid description of both the current and the desired culture.

- Visit two other successful Deans that you know for a day or two. See how they have organized their office and their personnel.

- Read a book or two on becoming a dean. A valuable quick read is: *"Pearls: For Leaders in Academic Medicine"* by Emery A. Wilson, Jay A. Perman, and D. Kay Clawson (publisher: Springer). It is only 68 pages – (sadly for the farsighted, it is published in very small font) – but packed with valuable suggestions and observations. A more in-depth, detailed academic leadership guide, albeit not School of Medicine specific, is the recently published *"From Ivory Tower to Glass House"* by Andrew J. Policano.

- Review your offer letter to make sure that in addition to those items specific to your ability to succeed at your given location, there are certain personal items that must be locked in:
    - ✓ Your salary should be pegged to an agreed upon AAMC percentile level. This will insure that it keeps pace with the times.
    - ✓ Incentives need to be specifically defined along with the exact rewards that would apply (e.g. moving up in the AAMC percentile level of compensation).
    - ✓ While it may seem premature, you need to have a guarantee as to what will happen when you **step down**, regardless of circumstances. This severance package might include a cash payout, a sabbatical guarantee, or both. The sabbatical is particularly helpful if you plan to remain at your institution after stepping down; it will provide you the necessary time to recover, regroup, and redirect.

If you are an internal "**interim**" (potentially permanent) dean tempest tossed into the position, you are about to undergo a precipitous metamorphosis. Here are some helpful steps:

- STOP all of your other activities (e.g. step away from committee meetings, put a hold on your clinical work, etc.) immediately; hopefully this will provide a 2- to 4-week cushion before you assume the full responsibility of being the interim dean.

- Sit with the outgoing dean to better understand what he or she saw as the biggest challenges, impediments to progress, strongest/weakest chairs based on their performance and their ability to see beyond their departmental needs to the benefit of the entire school/university, and most importantly who in the dean's office they would "rehire" if they were coming onboard.

- Reach out for guidance by connecting with former mentors or leaders at places where you have trained who may now be in a dean's role.

- Seek advice, albeit guardedly, from each of the associate deans in the School of Medicine as well as each of the chairs and center directors – with these individuals a "stop, start, continue" exercise (what are we doing that we should "stop", what aren't we doing that we should "start", what are we doing that we should "continue") may be very helpful in enabling you to develop an accurate snapshot of the School of Medicine. Realize these individuals still see you as an equal and you will have to earn their support/trust. (Caveat: Beware of the individual who upon your being announced as interim dean comes to congratulate you, tells you how happy they are because of your "promotion", let's you know that he (rarely she) lobbied strongly for you to get this position, and then wants to know what title in the dean's office you will be giving them. This is a person who likely wants your position and sees your ascent as the first stepping stone to their realizing a similar position. Don't bring this person into your leadership circle, as they will be an ongoing "leak" of sensitive information in an effort to augment their own standing among other chairs on campus. The easiest thing to do initially is to thank the person for their support and let them know that you are not planning to make any new appointments for at least the initial 4 months of your tenure so you can get your feet on the ground.)

- Push to have weekly or biweekly meetings with the executive vice chancellor and/or chancellor. You have been tapped because the School of Medicine is "in trouble"; you need to know their vision for the School of Medicine and what they believe specifically needs to be accomplished and in what order. By the same token, the leadership needs to be apprised as to the progress you are making and what, if any, roadblocks stand in your way. *Transparency builds trust*.

In contrast, if you are an interim, "place-holder", dean filling the position while a search is continuing, realize that no one is looking to you to become dean. Most large ships continue to move forward even after the engines have been silenced. Look at this as a sabbatical. Your job is to not rock the boat; nor should you expect that you are going to receive any "fuel" to actually move the boat forward beyond its engines-off "coasting speed".

(Author's note: Most wars, both civil and world, occur over a 4-5 year span. Rare is the leader who swims well in both waters, as each requires its own set of specialized skills. Determine whether you are being hired to be a *war time* or a *peace time* dean by answering three questions:

1. Is the School of Medicine in the black?
2. Is the School fully accredited by the LCME (i.e., no areas in transition or out of compliance)?
3. Do 90% of the departments within the School have a full time, non-interim chair?

If the answer to all three questions is "yes", then the campus is likely at "peace" – politics, negotiations and building on the status quo will prevail. You will have the luxury of time for reflection as you gently move the entity forward. Longevity is likely. If the answer to any two of these questions is "no", then you are likely in a "war" scenario demanding bold strokes and accelerated decision making. The work load is multiplied as are the expectations of the President and Chancellor. Longevity is uncertain.)

4. FIRST THINGS FIRST: (CONGRATULATIONS YOU GOT THE JOB, NOW WHAT?)

There are **12 tasks to accomplish within the first 12 weeks** after your appointment is announced, provided you are not a "place-holder" dean. (If you are truly in a caretaker position, there is no reason to upset the other passengers on the boat, especially since you will soon go from pilothouse to below decks to rejoin your colleagues.)

1. **Arrival**: Plan to arrive on campus 2-4 weeks BEFORE your start date so you can "settle in" and set up your office. You can also walk the campus and get a better feel for it.
2. **Personnel**: (if you have not done so already) create a campus personnel notebook either on your computer or as a ring-binder hard copy with name, title, contact, background, and photograph of each of the following stakeholders:
    *   **University campus leadership**: Chancellor, Executive Vice Provost, Chief Financial Officer for the University, Chief Communications person for the University, Chief of Advancement, Assoc. Executive Vice Chancellor (in charge of personnel), Chief Legal Counsel, malpractice counsel, current head of the academic senate, Chair of promotions and tenure committee)
    *   **School of Medicine Leadership**: Vice Deans, Assoc. Deans, Chief Compliance Officer, Chief Administrative Officer, and Chief Financial Officer for the School of Medicine, President of the Physicians' Practice Plan, head of advancement for the School of Medicine, head of communications for the School of Medicine, chief of the

billing group, President of the Medical Staff, Chief Legal Counsel for the School of Medicine, Chair of Space and Resource Allocation Committee(s)

- **Hospital Leadership**: Chief Executive Officer, Chief Operating Officer, Chief Strategy Officer, Chief Medical Officer, Chief Nursing Officer, Chief Financial Officer, Chief Information Officer, senior director of government healthcare programs (University's political liaison)
- **Department Chairs and Center Directors** (e.g. Cancer Center, Digestive Disease Center, etc.)
- **Deans of other schools on campus that interact with the School of Medicine** (e.g. Biological Sciences, Engineering, etc.)
- **Board Members**
- **Extramural individuals of importance**: state and county legislators, mayors of cities in your catchment area, community supporters/donors, Chief Executive Officers of affiliate hospitals (e.g. VAH, private hospitals, county hospitals)

3. **Personnel**: Interview all stakeholders (vide supra #2), *in their offices* if possible, and seek their thoughts on current successes (best programs and best people in the school), current problems and potential solutions (if you could change one thing in the school, what would it be? One practical and one blue sky task), what can you do to make their lives better, and how do they define the culture of the school. These interviews can be set up for just 20 minutes each. Alternatively, you can make this a "stop, start, continue" exercise. The composite picture from all the respondents will provide a vivid picture of the current culture. You need to be completely on "intake" mode (transmitter off, receiver on). *LISTEN! LISTEN! LISTEN! ...and promise nothing!* (Vide infra: #12)

4. **Personnel**: Hire and retain a GREAT personal assistant. This is the person who will make or break your life. Spare no expense in seeking and hiring this individual. Vet this person well. Regardless of stated references, also call prior employers, their penultimate employer as this individual's recommendation is not colored by perhaps their desire to see the applicant "move on". Also, a "temp" agency is an excellent way to try out a personal assistant. While pricey, you can change these individuals on a monthly basis if you so desire until you find an assistant who is truly simpatico and highly effective/efficient; it will cost you extra dollars to hire

that person away from the temp agency, but you will have a "known" talent. This is the one person who can and should make you appear "better" than you are and ease your burden significantly. In sum, a great personal assistant is worth her/his weight in platinum.

Also, once hired, expend the effort to retain this individual. In this regard, one dean noted the value of sending your administrative assistant each year to the meeting of the Dean's Assistants Group (DAG); this is both a reward for a job well done and a source of helpful networking.

(Caveat: When you come into the Dean's office you will invariably inherit the prior dean's personal assistant. Over the next two months, you need to decide if this individual shares your "cultural" vision and responds well to your style of leadership. If not, move him/her out and seek someone who does.)

5. **Personnel**: Hire a GREAT Chief of Staff – outstanding people draw outstanding people into the dean's office. Your office staff defines "you" and can reinforce your cultural aspirations.

6. **Space**: Walk the floor. *WALK EVERY SQUARE FOOT of space that is allotted to the School of Medicine.* There should be no building or space that you control to which you have not paid a visit within the first 12 weeks. Create a book with clear designation of all of your research, teaching, and clinical space; for *research space* indicate the investigator to whom the space is assigned and review the annual grant dollars/square foot on a running three year basis. Space visits should be unannounced so you see them as they are – you may be surprised by how much space is vacant or underutilized. Also, you need to *visit all of your practice sites* – both on campus and off-campus and learn whether they are hospital based (site of service 22 – the hospital's responsibility) or office based (site of service 11 – your responsibility). If you are Vice Chancellor for Health then you are responsible for both kinds of practices.

7. **Finances**: Take the time to learn about the school's finances. Sit with your CFO weekly to learn about the school's budget and each department's fiscal status. If after 4 weeks of these meetings, you are ill at ease, consider having an outside agency audit the books – you don't want to inherit someone else's fiscal mess and the best way to avoid that is to have an outside audit so you, and everyone from the Chancellor on down, knows from where you are beginning. On Day ONE, you inherit all that preceded you.

8. **Training**: If possible attend 1-2 LCME site visits at other schools as an observer, so you begin to understand the accreditation process. *You NEED this knowledge.*

9. **Training**: Plan to attend the two-part "new deans" sessions given by the AAMC (January and June). The pair of courses covers a broad range of topics; it also provides an introduction to a "class" of deans who are at a similar point in their career. If you start your deanship in July, then plan to take the pair of courses beginning in January, before "patterns" are established at your institution.

10. **Training**: Visit one or two successful deans (i.e. in the position for at least 5 years) at another medical school similar in size and nature to your own.

11. **Strategy**: Toward the end of your introductory period, when you have a handle on the culture, begin to embark on a strategic planning exercise. If you have the talent in-house (i.e. a business school that can provide this service) to do this, then use it, if not, seek outside expertise (e.g. AMC Strategies www.amcstrategies.com). Beware of individuals extolling their ability to create a strategic plan in a weekend (along with a complementary container of snake oil) – this will not succeed as *you need BUYIN from all of your stakeholders. Plan on this exercise taking 3-12 months.* Realize that "winning the war" is often easier than "winning the peace" and there are many strategic plans that get written but never implemented. To implement your strategic plan, you need both faculty champions and tactic-targeted funding.

12. **Transitions**: Change *absolutely nothing.* Let people know that you need to get yourself settled over the next 12 weeks – you need time to assess and deliberate. (In the mold of Abraham Lincoln: "I walk slowly, but I never walk backward.") This will provide people with some security and allow you the time to interview all of the stakeholders in order to better know the culture and complete your own SWOT (strengths, weaknesses, opportunities, and threats) analysis of the School of Medicine. Develop a three-tiered Fix It book based on your stakeholder interviews (vide supra #3): *fix now, fix soon, fix later.*) Proceed to act on the easiest, least disruptive *"fix now"* item *in your third month* so people can point to a positive action that has occurred since you became dean.

Table 1: Checklist for a New Dean: 12 things to do in the first 12 weeks

	1.	Arrival	2-4 weeks before your official start date
	2.	Personnel	Create a campus personnel guide: photograph, name, title, phone, email of all stakeholders.
	3.	Personnel	20 minute interview with each person in your campus personnel guide *in their office*
	4.	Personnel	Hire a first rate personal assistant (spare no expense in this endeavor)
	5.	Personnel	Hire a first rate Chief of Staff (spare no expense in this endeavor)
	6.	Space	Walk every square foot of your designated research, teaching, and clinical space (site of service 11 and 22/office space and hospital space). (Note areas without any activity). Create a source book with all space under the purview of the School of Medicine. For research space, note lead researcher in each laboratory and the dollars in grant support per square foot on a running 3 year average.
	7.	Finances	Finances 101 – set up weekly meetings with your Chief Financial Officer and use this as a tutorial to learn the nuances of the school's finances – Consider an independent audit of the school's finances.
	8.	Training	Attend a LCME site visit at another school.

9.	Training	Plan to attend the two "new deans" sessions given by the AAMC (January and June)
10.	Training	Visit one or two successful deans (i.e. in the position for at least 5 years) at another school similar in size and nature to your own. Learn from them.
11.	Strategic Planning	Begin plans for a strategic plan exercise to start later into your first year.
12.	Transition	*Sloth* – for the initial 12 weeks make few if any terminations or appointments to the dean's office. Focus on one "easy" highly visible fix.

During your first 3 months, everyone will want to meet the new dean. Attend all events to which you are invited provided they have completed the form in Appendix II; a prerequisite for your attendance should be the opportunity to address the audience preferably at the outset of the event/dinner. Let people know how excited you are to be the new Dean and that you are actively seeking to learn about the campus and its culture. Be prepared to paint a broad very positive vision in the most general terms. *Attend, speak, eat the salad and leave!*

5. ORGANIZATION AND INFRASTRUCTURE

Resist the temptation to please some faculty by immediately adding new titles with the word "dean" in them to your leadership group. Instead declare a moratorium on new appointments for your first 3 months (i.e. your "buffering" period). Another way to brake the clamoring for a position in your administration is to require that all of your Senior Associate Deans devote a minimum of 70-80% of their time to their work in the Dean's office. This rule discourages title-seekers while providing you with committed individuals who will get the "work" done (at least they should have the time to do the work!). Also, it will still allow them to continue to work within their given department thereby providing you with several "ears to the ground" that can communicate important information regarding the overall campus' vital signs and the faculty's opinion of your leadership. Certainly there are exceptions to this advice especially if there are posts in the dean's office that are vacant. Still the advice is to move s---l---o---w---l---y.

One controversial post is that of **Vice Dean**. In this regard there are two strategies. First there can be a Vice Dean that serves as the Dean's right arm and surrogate and who is a part of all high level discussions and decisions and serves as the first point of contact for department chairs and center directors (similar to serving as Vice President of a government organization). This approach is a two-edged sword. On the one edge, this person will insulate you from the chairs and center directors and thus cut you loose to take a more visionary stance as you seek out new opportunities. On the other edge, this person will blunt your contact with the chairs and center directors and you risk becoming out of touch with the very organization you are seeking to lead. The alternative approach is to use the title of Vice Dean similar to the way Vice President is used in the corporate world wherein there commonly are multiple Vice Presidents. In this case Vice Dean would be the same as the title of Senior Associate Dean in other schools and comes with markedly decreased powers.

Given the described concerns, it is not surprising that only one-fourth of the responding deans appointed a Vice Dean. Among the few deans who did, they noted that it was important for this person to be a more senior individual who is a veteran at the institution (i.e. 20 or more years of service), knows the history of the institution and has a track record for providing sage advice. This person needs to be well organized, credible, well-respected by the faculty, trustworthy to a fault, and loyal to the Dean. You can assign this individual some very broad responsibilities such as managing space requests and being the direct report for department chairs, center directors and even some of your associate deans

There are certain organizational commonalities for all medical schools with regard to personnel in the dean's office. These positions include:

- Chief Financial Officer;
- Research leader (this post may include research training as well as innovation);
- Clinical leader;
- Academic/promotions personnel (i.e., for faculty, an Associate Dean for Faculty Affairs and for office staff, a Chief of Staff);
- Educational leader.

Also in today's environment, many organizations are seeking to create joint appointments in order to better integrate the medical school with the physician's practice plan (e.g. the head of the practice plan also holds the title of Assoc. Dean for Clinical Operations in the School of Medicine) and with the hospital (e.g. the Chief Medical Officer is also given the title of Assoc. Dean for Clinical Affairs in the School of Medicine while the Chief Strategy Officer and Chief Information Officer are provided a dual report to the CEO and the Dean).

There are **other posts** that many deans have found helpful. The most common among these is a post that focuses on the community and governmental/political issues. To be sure, a common growing theme among medical schools beyond the traditional research, education and clinical missions is one of community service/social justice. There are various titles for this job: Vice Chancellor for Community Health, Senior Associate Dean for Health Policy, Associate Senior Vice Chancellor for Political Strategy, or Associate Dean for Community and Culture. The job description includes: informing/advising the Dean on local, state and federal healthcare policies and strategies as well as being the Dean's representative to churches, cultural organizations, the mayor's office, and the county/city precollege school system. This position may be divided into two: one strictly political/governmental and the other devoted to all nonpolitical/nongovernmental aspects of the community (e.g. churches, high schools, elementary schools, cultural groups, etc.).

The following list consists of largely **one-off unique positions** in the dean's office:

- Special projects: Assistant Dean for Executive Affairs or Assistant Dean of Special Projects: This is a utility infielder nonMD nonPhD person who provides the necessary added bandwidth to organize special events on campus as well as spearhead new Dean's initiatives. This person works closely with advancement.

- Education:
  - o Special Education Consultant to the Dean: This is an individual with extensive knowledge of LCME accreditation and guidelines whose responsibility is to aid compliance with all of the LCME criteria and prepare for the periodic LCME site visit through ongoing updating of the necessary files and tracking documents.
  - o Sr. Assoc. Dean for Professional Education Programs (CME): This person is responsible for all CME courses and other educational offerings. In many schools this position reports to the Senior Associate Dean for Education.

- Research: President of the Medical Science Foundation: This is a 501c (3) that exists outside the University primarily to support the school's research and to a lesser extent, the school's educational activities. This organization provides support for those activities that may otherwise be restricted due to lack of funding from the usual sources (e.g. grants) that lie within the university.

- Clinical: Executive Physician in Chief/Chief Strategy Officer: This person helps with re-engineering the clinical enterprise and strategizing on the development of supportive clinical networks.

- Faculty development/wellness:
  - o Associate Dean for Faculty Affairs or Director of the Institute of Professional Development and Leadership: This person develops mentorship programs and provides learning experiences for the faculty in leadership, philanthropy and finance along with a special emphasis on diversity (gender, ethnicity, etc.). In some schools there is a separate position for an Associate Dean for Diversity.
  - o Director of Spiritual Life and Wholeness: This faculty member is an advocate who can reach out from the Dean's office to troubled or "at risk" faculty, residents, fellows, or medical students.

- Industry relations: Associate Dean for Corporate Development: This individual, who has a MBA and entrepreneurial experience, establishes industry contacts with faculty and helps shepherd the resulting contracts and agreements through the university. These agreements may include the rental of medical school laboratory space to industry, industry consulting agreements with the school/faculty, and/or industry support for teaching or research.
- Global health: Senior Vice Chancellor for International Relations: This individual is responsible for developing international liaisons for education and research as well as for promoting the university's clinical programs.

6. CULTURE

"The wrong culture can never institute the right strategic plan!"

Culture, strategic plan development, and strategic plan implementation are the three **sequential** steps to success. Simply stated: "culture eats strategy." So first develop an understanding of the campus culture based on your stakeholder interviews. If the culture is right, then it is time to proceed with strategic planning; however, if the culture is in need of change then initiate this work before getting into the strategic planning process.

There are only three "T" levers that you have as dean to impact on the campus culture: talent (people –titles - interpersonal relationships), treasure (unrestricted funds from taxes, endowments, etc.), and territory (distribution of space with the medical school). Of note, albeit not surprising, among the three levers, according to the respondents, *talent* is paramount as it is the dean's interpersonal relations with each of the gifted stakeholders and the ability to build a skilled support system that will ultimately determine success. To be sure, that talent is best served and preserved by the sage use of treasure and territory.

What culture is most conducive to creating a successful strategic plan? Among the respondents, the most common cultural goal noted was *collaboration* (also described as inclusiveness/collegiality/mutual respect/family). Collaboration rather than internal competition was seen as the preferred means for attaining excellence. The end product of a successful collaborative culture was that of an all-encompassing sense of a campus-wide "family"; the *sine qua non* for this to occur relied on ALL people on the campus having a proactive spirit of treating each other with *respect, trust, kindness, and selflessness.*

(Author's note: This brings into view the concept of "academic mathematics", whereby: $1 + 1 \neq 2$, instead $1 + 1 =$ either 0 or 3, dependent upon whether the atmosphere is one of collaboration, a "3", or one of competitive infighting, a "0".)

Following "collaboration" were several other cultural characteristics (in order): "exceptional clinical care", "scholarship", "innovation" and "transparency". Of note, there were also several intriguing cultural one offs provided by the respondents: trust, accountability, excellence, safety, service, and philanthropy. Regarding the last two, it was stressed by one dean, that "in order to be valued by the community, the members of the school needed to be *of value to the community*." The measure of community support can be gauged by patient referrals as well as philanthropy.

The next challenge is how to either **maintain a positive culture or reconfigure a negative culture** on your campus? This question provided a rich array of suggestions:

a. **Consultants**: The end product of such an engagement should include the definition of the current versus the desired culture on your campus and provide a roadmap for either maintenance or transformation. The following firms were recommended: Seen Delaney, Disney Institute, and Quint Studer.

b. **Develop pride in ownership**: Create a history display on your campus with posters that define your culture based on specific past achievements which are supportive of your desired culture and mission. This can take the form of a traveling exhibit (e.g. for display at campus wide or community events) with a replica or housing of the original exhibit displayed prominently in the Vice Chancellor's/Dean's office. In celebrating specific highlights of your past you acknowledge the culture that existed at that time, thereby implying your intent to maintain or re-establish that culture.

c. **Enculturation sessions for all new members to your campus**: Without a formal enculturation process, each new recruit/student *dilutes the culture*. Rather than leaving new recruits to "discover" your culture in a "catch as catch can" manner, it is far better to clearly describe it to them in detail upon their arrival. For incoming medical students and residents this becomes part of their orientation training. For new faculty, a two day program can be initiated; this should occur within the first week of their employment (Appendix III) and involve all of the leadership in the dean's and CEO's offices as well as the Vice Chancellor/dean and CEO, themselves. *Do not delegate this to someone else.*

d. **Leadership** *("A leader knows the way, shows the way, and goes the way." —John C. Maxwell)*: The Vice Chancellor/Dean and CEO should re-enforce the core mission/vision/values (i.e. the culture of the institution) at every opportunity. Speeches should begin or end with the mission statement, the vision statement, as well as specific examples addressing the institutional values. Progress reports should be given such that they are divided clearly among each of the mission areas. The leadership is the role model for the culture and is responsible for creating an environment with a common sense of pride in the tradition, the present, and the future of the institution. If you don't live your culture, nobody else will.

e. **Ceremonies and celebrations**: Praise accomplishments and their owners at every opportunity. Success needs to be CELEBRATED. If there are set backs, the dean takes responsibility for the failure, seeks the root cause, and creates new pathways that will empower faculty to succeed while closing off the paths that led to the failure. Never miss an opportunity to celebrate your people and their successes.

f. **Corrective actions**: Cultural transgressions need to be addressed expeditiously so that corrective action ensues promptly. Failure to do so will negate any positive reinforcement activity and will ultimately drive away individuals of excellence and good will. These actions may include *counseling,* anger management courses, training in professionalism, or termination from a position of leadership. Although not seeking lawsuits, you cannot be cowed into inaction by the threat of their likelihood.

g. **Enlightened hiring**: Be sure that each new major hire (department chair, center director, leadership position) shares the culture that you want to establish/maintain at your institution. This should be clearly stated in their offer letter along with a clear direction that your expectation is for them to uphold and promote the institution's mission/culture (vide infra: Chapter 9). If you hire chairs that embrace your culture, they in turn will bring new faculty onto campus who similarly share the institutional values and culture.

h. **Departmental annual report**: In addition to the usual data on grants, publications, resident test scores, clinical activity, revenue, etc., there should be a section of the report on *how the department is fulfilling the institutional mission, values, and vision within the context of the campus' culture*. Each chair needs to clearly understand that their responsibility is to make not just their department, but the school and the hospital as good as they can be. They need to contribute to the rising tide that lifts the entire institution.

i. **Dean's luncheon**: Another suggestion to enforce the institution's culture was to create a chairs only, dean's luncheon; this would occur as often as every month or as infrequently as annually. At this luncheon, one chair would be selected to present his /her department's and faculty's accomplishments as well as how the department is contributing to the campus culture while ministering to the institutional mission, values, and vision.

j. **Annual peer-chair evaluation**: Each year, each chair is asked to anonymously evaluate each of the other chairs using a simple one page form which includes the following metrics: collegiality, institutional commitment, and overall effectiveness. These evaluations become part of each chair's annual performance evaluation as reviewed by the Vice Chancellor/Dean.

k. **Student admissions**: As one dean noted: "The admissions committee is the single most important committee to assure long term survival of the mission of the medical school." The school needs to select students who are aligned with your culture and mission. In this regard, the culture/mission/vision/values of your institution should be highlighted in the medical school brochure and on the website.

l. **Advertising**: If possible (i.e. a brief mission statement), place your school's mission on lapel pins, license plate holders, slide templates or other knick-knacks (e.g. coffee mugs, caps, etc.) and widely, and freely, distribute these items to incoming students, residents, fellows, staff, and faculty.

m. **Stationery, business cards and email**: Each of these should have your tagline (or alternatively your mission, vision, values or culture statement) incorporated somewhere on the page or within your signature block.

n. **Mission based dean's letter** (electronic, hard copy or both): This communication can be organized on the basis of your mission and sent out every 2 to 4 weeks or quarterly, chronicling the accomplishments of the faculty, staff, and students in each of the mission-based/cultural areas. It is also an opportunity to highlight your community supporters.

o. **Create a Leadership Development Institute**: The members of the institute, which may number in the hundreds, and include faculty, staff, students, residents, and fellows meet 3 times a year to review progress in maintaining or developing the culture and to determine goals for the coming year. Tasks completed are noted and the responsible parties recognized; new tasks are defined and accountable parties are enrolled. This also provides the Vice Chancellor/Dean with a chair's leadership evaluation management tool in that specific institutional leadership goals become part of each department chair's performance evaluation.

p. **Hard wiring the culture into the leadership**: Have everyone on your leadership council read and sign a "leadership compact" that contains the key elements of your mission and culture. Subsequently, at each meeting of your leadership council, begin with one member providing a 5 minute reflection on one element of the leadership compact with a brief discussion to follow (move down the mission/vision/values/culture list in alphabetical order at subsequent meetings).

q. **Mentorship**: All new hires into the School of Medicine are assigned a "culturally-astute" mentor. The mentor is determined well in advance of the new faculty member's arrival and the name of the mentor and contact information are included in the offer letter such that the "relationship" begins well in advance of the new faculty member's physical presence on campus.

7. STRATEGIC PLAN: FORMULATION AND IMPLEMENTATION

"If you don't know where you are going any road will take you there."
−Lewis Carroll

The **strategic plan** is a manifestation of the culture of the institution. Once you understand and wish to promote the current culture of the institution or have determined the type of culture change that is necessary for the institution to progress and have made sufficient progress toward that end, then the time is ripe for formulating a strategic plan. As an outgrowth of the culture, the strategic plan contains the defined *values* of the institution which informs the institution's *mission* (what your school exemplifies regardless of what ever challenges may unfold) and the institution's *vision* (what your school will achieve if it remains true to its mission). Within the strategic plan is a measurable, metric based roadmap replete with the specific strategies and attendant tactics necessary for achieving the visionary themes. It is key to keep both the mission statement and the vision statement sufficiently simple in order to *reinforce* them each time you, as dean, are given an opportunity to speak. One dean noted that at every event, the mission and vision statements were woven into their comments, usually at the beginning or end of their talk, specific to the audience that was being addressed (e.g. faculty, board, community members, or medical students).

A well-organized strategic plan contains themes (aspirations in each of the areas vital to the institution – education, research, community service, clinical affairs, etc.) which in turn are subdivided into specific goals (measurable milestones to determine progress). Each goal is supported by a series of actionable strategies (broad albeit definitive activities regarding the method for achieving the goal) which in turn are supported by a series of highly specific metric-based tactics. The tactics are detailed, practical tasks with well-defined budgets and expected outcomes which undergo a scheduled review (e.g. quarterly). (An example of a color coded chart (i.e. red-failure, yellow-near miss, green-accomplished) for monitoring tactical progress is provided in Appendix IV.)

Few of the decanal respondents noted any formal training in strategic planning prior to entering the dean's office; yet over 95% noted that developing a strategic plan for their School of Medicine was a prominent part of their job description. How did they do it?

The majority tackled this challenge either as an in-house endeavor (53%) or with the aid of a hired facilitator (25%); the exception was to employ an outside strategic planning consulting group. Which of the three paths to take is very much dependent upon whether or not you have inherited a working strategic plan or you are truly starting from scratch with the need to develop a strategic plan that will foster and sustain a major shift in culture.

If your organization already has had successful past strategic plans developed and implemented, then a simple 1- to 2-day retreat may be sufficient to review and revise the old plan. This can be done with or without a facilitator or consultant depending on the amount of work that needs to be done and the perceived level of current faculty satisfaction. By the same token, if prior strategic plans are available to you, it is helpful to review them; time taken to determine what was or wasn't implemented can be very informative.

Alternatively, if a major overhaul of a pre-existing strategic plan is required, then a more extensive in-house approach is pursued. Specifically, four working groups (research, education, clinical, and community service) are established with each co-chaired by the vice-dean/senior associate dean specific to each area and an "elected" faculty representative plus a hand-picked group of area-specific stakeholders. Their charge is to develop the themes, goals, strategies, tactics, and metrics in their assigned area within the known constraints of the institution's values, mission and vision. At a later specified date, the full complement of co-chairs assembles to review and stitch together into a single document, the plans that have been developed in each area, following which, the plan is presented to the leadership/strategic planning committee for further discussion and refinement.

The aforedescribed is a best case scenario in which prior strategic plans have been developed and implemented and the entire strategic planning/implementation process is embedded within the culture of the institution. However, if you are at an institution where no definable strategic plan currently exists or strategic plans have been developed but never implemented, or your institution is in a state of turmoil, retaining an outside academic strategic planning consulting group, although expensive, may be optimal (Appendix V: Recommended Agencies). This action sends an immediate message to all faculty and staff that this strategic planning endeavor is not the "same old, same old" futile exercise. Also the consultants can facilitate cutting through what one dean termed: "the academic debate society where you can never get closure." Expect this kind of a strategic plan exercise to take upwards of 12 months to complete. The cost of involving a formal agency over the year necessary to develop a strategic plan for your campus is in the $400,000 - $500,000 range. However, with a *bona fide* strategic planning consulting group (i.e. one that you have vetted with other deans) you will most definitely obtain a functional strategic plan.

It is key to ensure that, regardless of the method selected, the process, embraces all stakeholders and evolves in a transparent manner at every step along the way. As one dean noted: "Traditional approaches are suspect in the current climate of volatility, uncertainty, complexity, and ambiguity." The strategic plan steering committee (up to 40 members) should include the key leadership from the hospital, along with the department chairs and center directors. Additional individuals to include might be a representative from each affiliated hospital, one or two community members (major supporters/donors), the chair of the academic senate, chair of the board or a representative from the Chancellor's office, as well as a medical student (possibly the president and/or vice president of the senior class or of each class), a resident, and a graduate student.

Transparency during all phases of the strategic plan development is of the utmost importance, as it engenders faculty trust in the process. It is the surest way of obtaining widespread support for the second phase of the endeavor, that being implementation. Transparency is best achieved by (1) seeking input from the entire faculty, staff, and other stakeholders (community leaders, board members, students, residents, fellows, etc.); this can be done via a computer-based questionnaire disseminated across the institution at the very beginning of the strategic planning process; and (2) creating a perpetually updated Strategic Plan website that can be accessed by all faculty and staff.

Creation of a strategic plan is merely the "*end of the beginning*". You need to have the energy and the finances to implement the plan. As one dean aptly put it: "I purposely chose not to have a strategic planning exercise as we had a history of doing such and then paying no attention to the massive resulting slide deck which only led to faculty and staff cynicism."

Although the dean can assign *ownership* to each of the various strategies to be implemented, the assignment must be accompanied by the earmarking of dollars to support the specific tactics necessary to achieve the chosen strategies. The strategic plan steering committee and the various strategy co-champions need to be aware of the total number of dollars being committed to the strategic plan each year. The champions of each goal-oriented strategy and the results (i.e., metrics) for each strategy need to be posted on an institution-wide website and should also be presented at specific strategic planning meetings throughout the year when the entire membership of the steering committee and the leadership are present. The "go to green" charts are a clear indication of the plan's progress and the individuals making it progress (Appendix IV).

Ultimately, the success or failure of the strategic plan comes down to faculty leadership and accountability. To that end, several deans noted that in order to implement the plan, beyond hard work and "nudging," a reasonably low threshold for leadership change was important. Simply put, leaders of a given strategy who do not deliver, despite well-funded tactics, need to be replaced; indeed, the replacement of one or two leaders often sends a clear signal that funding of tactics mandates accountability.

Given that the bandwidth of individuals at each institution is often narrow and, in the minds of each faculty member, perpetually exceeded, the organization and monitoring of a full-blown strategic plan requires two dedicated individuals: one to manage the plan and one to oversee its progress. The former should have a minimum of 50% time to devote to plan maintenance. This individual has the responsibility for managing the strategic plan: (1) updating the plan website; (2) collecting and collating the quarterly reports from the leaders of the various strategies (e.g., in one plan, there were seven themes with 14 goals and 33 supporting strategies—each strategy had a pair of co-leaders, who were responsible for reporting on the funding and progress of the tactics in their area); (3) planning the various meetings with both leadership and the co-champions/strategic planning committee during the year; and (4) reporting to the designated strategic plan overseer. The overseer of the strategic plan typically will be the Chief Strategy Officer, the director of the Office of Information Management, or the Associate Dean for Executive Affairs. This individual works in concert with the plan manager and is directly responsible for reporting on the progress in implementation to the dean/leadership. A caveat: although clearly, the plan will be successful only if the dean is fully committed to it, the dean would be ill-advised to accept the role of overseer personally. As one dean lamented regarding his institution's strategic plan: "It is in need of update now, and I've been trying to develop measures and metrics for all of our themes and goals to make it more dynamic—to develop a dashboard. Have been overcome by curriculum redesign right now."

Furthermore, to facilitate implementation of the strategic plan, several deans commented on the importance of *constant review and adjustments*. This becomes a dynamic process that occurs in the dean's office on a daily or weekly basis and is a designated topic for each cabinet meeting. Indeed, the dean's task list may be incorporated into the strategic plan so the two are congruent. As such, for cabinet meetings, tactics and strategies specific to the strategic plan that "live" in the dean's office can be reviewed. Along these lines, one approach is to have, on a quarterly basis, one of the four mission leaders (i.e., research, education, clinical, community/philanthropy) present a review of their mission area. Also, keeping an up-to-date grid of the entire strategic plan provides the dean with a current snapshot of how all projects are progressing and alerts the dean to any problems, especially those deliverables for which the dean's cabinet members (e.g., senior associate deans) may be either wholly or partly responsible. In this regard, it is valuable for the school's information technology staff to develop or perhaps purchase a dynamic software program to allow the strategic plan manager to update the plan continually and provide integration with departments, centers, institutes, and the dean's office's functional areas.

Campus-wide meetings to review the strategic plan typically occur annually (69% of the respondents). However a more frequent schedule may be followed dependent upon how far along the school is with regard to implementing the strategic plan. In contrast, strategic plan-focused meetings by the executive planning committee (i.e., the key leadership of the academic health center) with and without the goal-specific strategy leaders may be scheduled on a quarterly or semi-annual basis, depending on: the complexity of the strategic plan, the urgency of its implementation, and the progress being made with each tactic (i.e., updated go-to-green charts, funding challenges, personnel changes). These meetings are organized by the strategic plan manager; they provide an annual forum for the co-champions to request funding for their tactics and an opportunity for the leadership to inform the strategy champions as to which of their proposed tactics will be funded for the coming year. A comprehensive meeting schema for strategic plan implementation and review is provided in Appendix VI.

By the same token, as you are requiring progress reports from each of the plan's subgroups, you should also have a *set recurring time* to provide the Chancellor/Provost/Board with an annual progress report. This should be a face-to-face meeting with prior submission of a formal report with the various dashboards and details of how funds were invested. This is your moment to determine how much your school has accomplished in each area over the past year.

Lastly, a formal review and overhaul of the strategic plan is usually conducted every 3 to 5 years. This is arranged by the strategic plan manager and the strategic plan overseer. Alternatively, an outside agency with whom you have previously worked on your strategic plan can revisit your campus and lead the review. An added benefit of having the plan consultants return to campus is their ability to provide a backdrop against which the progress of the plan can be gauged on the basis of their experience with peer medical schools across the country.

Suggestion: One dean hired a communications firm to develop an "elevator speech" for their strategic plan and to create key bullet points that could be consistently used in all communications. This is one way to help move the organization to better understand and support not only the strategic plan but also the culture that the plan is seeking to sustain/introduce.

8. MARKETING AND BRANDING

"In days of competition, it pays to advertise." –Anonymous

It is important to separate marketing from branding as the first has to do with selling your organization to others whereas branding has to do with how your institution conceptually makes your constituency "feel". Marketing should be considered only after you have completed your strategic plan and the campus culture truly embraces your values, mission, goals, and vision.

At this point you might consider creating a "First, Best, and Only" brochure to promote your academic health center. Specifically what have your school's achievements been that were the first of their kind to be done. Likewise at what disciplines are you "best" of class (regionally, state-wide, or nationally) and what services do you offer that can "only" be obtained at your medical center (again this can be on a regional, state-wide, or national level). This kind of promotional material is easily created in a tri-fold card that can be distributed at campus or foundation events.

Overall half of the respondents had participated in a marketing or branding exercise, most often directed by the clinical practice leadership. The two most highly recommended firms {i.e. rating of 5 on a scale of 0 (lowest) to 5 (highest)} were: SPM Marketing &Communication and Munn Rabot; two other firms received a 4 rating: Miramar Communication and Capstrat (Raleigh, NC). Several deans noted that while the overall consulting engagement was not excessively expensive (in the $100,000 range), similar to the strategic plan, the implementation often ran into the millions of dollars.

The other half of the respondents were much less enthusiastic about the value of a branding or marketing exercise. Comments included:

> "Trying to brand our school is impossible…too many entities that make up the SOM with several doing their own branding exercise."

> "We have had many attempts to brand and market our school. It is debatable whether any of the efforts and the costs involved were truly justified since the outcome from any of these efforts never met expectations. There is no magic bullet."

Overall it seems that one needs to have a well-defined culture and a supportive strategic plan BEFORE an effective marketing or branding exercise should be considered. A premature attempt will likely be an unsatisfying waste of time and resources while potentially adversely affecting your institution's credibility, should you declare yourself to be something to which you aspire but have not yet become.

Caveat emptor

If you have your culture and strategy well in hand and elect to embark on a marketing or branding exercise, proceed with caution. As one dean noted: "Every vendor over promises what they can do." To avoid a disappointment here is a list of mission based metrics that can be used to determine if a marketing or branding exercise was indeed successful. It is worthwhile discussing these with the firm prior to hiring them to make sure they understand what you expect their work to ultimately produce.

1. **Research**: number of publications; cumulative impact factor of publications; number of National Institutes of Health (NIH) submissions; number of NIH awards; amount of NIH funding.

2. **Education**: Number of applicants to the medical school; median MCAT score of incoming class; median grade point average of incoming class; yield (class size/number of applicants accepted; anything > 50% is excellent); educational innovation awards from the Health Resources and Services Administration (HRSA).

3. **Clinical**: Number of patient encounters; number of patient referrals; market share; patient satisfaction score; number of operations (outpatient and inpatient); hospital

occupancy; clinical dollars realized; number of top-ranked programs.

4. **Other**: US News and World Report ranking; faculty retention rate; philanthropy—total dollars donated ([pledges > 5 years; pledges ≤ 5 years] and annual dollars realized [i.e., in the bank]); faculty climate survey scores; alumni survey scores; student survey scores; perception of department chairs; national faculty recognition awards (e.g., American Association for the Advancement of Science, Institute of Medicine, National Academy of Sciences, etc.); percent of medical students placed in top residency programs in their chosen field; percent of medical students matching into their first choice; percent of medical students matching on the first go-around; community "top of mind" survey.

9. HIRING AND NEGOTIATION: "WAIT FOR GREAT" (S. Smith: Corner Office interview: NY Times 12/14/14)

Creating a Productive Search Committee

A good beginning is vital to a good ending. The creation of an effective, collaborative search committee is essential when seeking to fill a departmental chair or center director's position. In this regard, the *chair of the search committee will very much define the success or failure of the search.* The consensus is that the chair of the committee should be a stakeholder department chair (i.e., chair of neurology if the search is for a neurosurgeon, chair of medicine if the search is for a family medicine chair). Similarly, if the search is for the chair of a basic science department, an individual with crossover interests from another basic science or research-oriented clinical department should run the search.

An alternative, albeit less common, approach is to have the Vice Dean (or Senior Assoc. Dean) for Academic Affairs head all search committees. The benefit of this approach is consistency in the process and the close involvement of the dean's office at every step of the way. However, one negative of this approach is loss of the utility of the chairing of the committee as a test of the leadership potential of a young chair.

In creating a search committee, it is important to seek a collaborative, fair, thoughtful, and reasonable group of individuals, usually no more than seven, although some deans described search committees of as many as 10 members. An alternative is to have only seven voting members and appoint several *ex-officio* members (e.g., community members, medical students, residents).

If the search is for a basic science chair, the majority of the members should be from the basic sciences but with at least one clinician with an interest in that area. In contrast, if the search is for a clinical chair, the majority of members should be clinicians with a least one basic scientist with an interest in that discipline. With this in mind, the professional composition of a clinical search committee invariably includes a member from each of the following groups: affiliated hospitals (especially the Veterans Affairs hospital), hospital leadership (e.g., COO, CMO, CNO, or CSO), a member from the faculty council/senate, and additional clinical/basic science faculty as previously noted. Among the responding deans, there was a strong consensus that the *clinical members should NOT come from the home department* but rather should be appointed on the basis of their being a nondepartmental stakeholder (e.g., a surgeon when the search is in anesthesiology). (Aside: Personal discretion is key here, as there may be a very senior member of the affected department whom you trust, that you would want on the search committee albeit not as chair.) In addition, some respondents noted they like to appoint to the committee a second departmental chair from another stakeholder department (e.g., for a search for a new chair of gynecology, one might consider having the chair of surgery head the search committee and also appoint to the committee the chair of urology or family medicine).

Other potential members of a clinical search committee, either voting or *ex officio*, may include a representative from the curriculum or graduate medical education committee, a medical student, a resident or a fellow, a community clinician in the specific discipline, nursing leadership, a member from the dean's office, and/or a community leader. The advantage of having a member from the dean's office is that it provides the dean with information as to how the committee is progressing as well as ensuring that the search is being done by the book.

For a basic science chair search, it is important to include both a graduate student and a member of the medical school's curriculum committee, given the importance of teaching in the basic sciences. Other potential members might include an individual from the campus grants office and the senior associate dean for research.

All search committees, regardless of task, need to be diverse both in sex and in racial/ethnic composition. One respondent noted that at their institution, a woman is always appointed as either Chair or Vice Chair of the committee. The Officer/Dean for Diversity can be helpful in reviewing the proposed committee and providing guidance to the Dean.

"Charging" the search committee

After selecting a search committee, the next step is to formally "charge" or activate it. This requires a visit from the dean to explain the rules under which the committee should proceed and the expected outcome. During that visit, you may wish to distribute a booklet that your office has prepared on conducting a search; this booklet should contain a confidentiality statement that each member of the search committee needs to sign and return to you, the logistics for first and second visits, information on unintended bias, and a clear statement as to the expectations for the committee, which is to perform a search and recommend candidates in alphabetical order for the position to the Dean, whereas the Dean's responsibility is actually to select the new chair. (Appendix VII)

There are eight steps one may elect to take in "charging" the search committee:

1. **Gravity of the endeavor**: Each member needs to know how seriously you view this endeavor and how much you appreciate their service to the school. Let them know the importance of moving forward with all due speed, that you expect that the committee will meet at least every two weeks, and that these meeting dates, on a specific day and at a specific time, should be set in advance for the next 6 months. Committee members who do not feel they will be able to attend these meetings need to be replaced before the search begins. Monthly decanal contact with the committee chair is important. Without this degree of organization, the committee may devolve into meetings with only half of its members present or possibly haphazard phone conferences; the search then is doomed.

2. **Confidentiality**: Confidentiality needs to be in perpetuity. The members need to know that any and all questions to them regarding the search should elicit the same answer: "The search is completely confidential. I am not allowed to discuss it. If you would like, I suggest you contact the Chair of the Search Committee." The question is to what level does one take this *sine qua non* directive? In this regard, 15% of the responding deans actually required all members of the search committee to sign a confidentiality statement. If you go this route, you need to back it up by dismissing any individual who refuses to sign the confidentiality statement or who subsequently violates the confidentiality agreement. With this in mind, it is of note that one respondent, while espousing the importance of confidentiality, noted with an air of disappointment: "…ask for confidentiality, but that never happens." It *must* happen.

3. **Planned logistics for the search**: Specifically detail the number and format for initial visits, subsequent visits, timeline for deliverables, and number of candidates the search committee is expected to put forward to the dean. First visits may be offered to five to eight candidates. When the number of candidates is in the seven to 15 range, many search committees consider doing either an airport screening without a formal visit to campus or a phone-call visit via Skype; the latter is far easier and provides the opportunity to vet a broad list of candidates rapidly.

   The candidate's first visit to campus is usually 1.5 days in length; you may wish to visit with the candidate on the first or wait until the second visit. A first visit interview, may enable you to eliminate those candidates with whom you have no chemistry, while others would argue there is no need for you to interact with individuals that the committee may rule out as semi-finalists, thus deferring your first interaction with the candidate to the second visit.

   While the first visit is limited to the candidate, the second visit often includes the candidate's spouse/family. With regard to the second visit, the search committee should never lose sight of the fact that they are recruiting *an entire family*. Taking the time to have the family come to campus, having the spouse interact with leadership spouses, and paying attention to special needs (e.g., schools in the area that would be appropriate for their children, senior centers if the individual will need to move with an elderly parent) may well make the difference between a successful and a failed search.

4. **Timeline**: The dean needs to provide the committee with a definite timeline for the completion of the work. Usually, this is 6 months.

5. **Knowledge of the department**: The committee needs to get to know the department for which they have been charged to find the new chair. In that regard, it is important for the dean's office to distribute to the committee the department's last annual report and to encourage a meeting between the faculty of that department and the committee chair, its members, or both.

6. **Diversity**: The committee at the outset needs basic training in the recognition and avoidance of unintended bias. It is helpful to have the faculty affairs or diversity director/associate dean address this aspect of the search with the committee. It is essential that the search committee develop a diverse pool of candidates based on gender and ethnicity.

7. **Number of candidates**: The committee needs to be instructed with regard to the number of candidates to present to the dean; typically this is two to four, listed in alphabetical order. Having them *unranked* is important, as nobody on the list wants to find out after they have been recruited, due to an unfortunate breach of confidentiality, that indeed, they were a second or third choice. Once the chair of the committee provides an unranked list of candidates, the committee's work is done, and the committee is disbanded.

8. **Administrative assistance**: The administrative assistance assigned to the committee is vital. To this end, it is recommended that the administrative staff of the dean's office directly assist the Chair of the Search Committee, rather than having this additional burden fall on the shoulders of the chair's administrative assistant. This arrangement ensures a degree of conformity in the search process and will increase the likelihood that each candidate will be treated well and equally. A dedicated individual from the dean's office should escort each candidate around campus to ensure they are on time for all appointments and do not get lost.

There are two other benefits of having a person from the dean's administrative staff directly interface with the candidate: (1) they can provide you with valuable insights about the candidate (e.g., are they on time, easily frazzled, organized, etc.) and (2) it will enhance the candidate's experience. Even if not selected, each candidate, if treated well, may serve as an advocate for your school and its faculty.

Developing the Candidate Pool

The identification of a proper candidate pool for a departmental chair or center director demands the dean's involvement. Two well-stated observations in this regard:

"Advertisements are worthless, except for documentation of the search…"

"My experience has been that essentially no viable candidates are identified through passive means such as advertisements."

This is where you, as Dean, will invariably be making your own bed; the culture you preach is no better than the congregants you hire. They need to be on the same page as you in order for the system to move forward smoothly. To be sure, you will be judged on the strength of the people you recruit and their subsequent accomplishments/longevity at your institution. The following steps are helpful in identifying great candidates:

1. **Faculty-generated candidates**: Meet with the affected department, and deputize the faculty to provide names of potential candidates to the search committee. Also, ask them to talk up the position at their national meetings in an effort to identify candidates.

2. **Don't ignore "home grown."** Indeed, if there is an individual that the faculty feel is capable of becoming the next chair, you should consider appointing that person as interim chair. Indeed, if the interim chair is a strong internal candidate, you may consider not appointing a search committee for 6 months to see if this individual is able to run the department to the satisfaction of the faculty and yourself; at the end of the 6 month period you, in concert with the faculty, can decide whether or not to proceed with a search. If the decision is to appoint the interim chair to the permanent position, then negotiations with that individual need to be undertaken in order to assure the faculty that hiring that person was not done out of expediency but out of prudence; the resulting chair package needs to reflect that same degree of respect and commitment as would be expended on an external candidate.

   (Terminology: Acting vs. interim. For the sake of simplicity the majority of respondents (2/3rds) favor using only the term "interim" regardless of the reason for a vacant chair. A few deans will use the term "acting" when a current chair is on sabbatical, ill, or has other circumstances resulting in a temporary absence. The "acting" chair is expected to maintain the status quo until the current chair returns from his/her absence. Alternatively, the term "acting" may be applied to an individual who is truly a "placeholder" for a vacated chair until a new chair can be recruited.)

3. **"Blue ribbon" review**: A leadership transition is the perfect time for you to conduct an outside in-depth review of the department. To form the blue ribbon committee, typically, two of the country's top department chairs in the specific discipline are invited to review the most recent departmental report and financial statement and then come to campus to interview faculty and stakeholders in the department. They then prepare a *SWOT* (strengths, weaknesses, opportunities, and threats) and *needs* analysis. In addition, they should include in the report individuals they think would be excellent candidates for the chair position according to both their analysis and who they feel would be a good fit, given the culture of your institution. This should be a paid consultation, not a favor, as a good report will require a considerable commitment of time and thought on the part of the two reviewers. This is money well spent and far less expensive than engaging a search firm.

4. **Seek out the BEST**. Look for the diamond in the rough. In trying to develop potential candidates, you, as the Dean, may elect to call the Chairs of the top 10-ranked departments in that specific discipline and ask them "Who you have trained or who do you believe is ready to become a chair?" *Resist the temptation to delegate this activity to the Chair of the Search Committee.* When you, as the Dean call, the reply is far different than if the head of the search committee calls. You can proceed to cross reference the various names that arise. Sometimes, to your surprise, the chair of one of these top 10 programs will offer herself/himself as a candidate. In this manner, you will likely generate upwards of five potential candidates that you can pass on to the chair of the search committee. These will most likely be individuals who have not applied for the position, and they will often be flattered when called to discuss a first interview.

5. **Seek diversity**. Your designated Associate Dean for Diversity should be part of each search process and should be responsible for providing you with two or three potential candidates. Although ads are always placed in the usual journals, you should also consider placing ads in

journals specifically addressing under-represented groups in medicine. You can also advertise through the Executive Leadership in Academic Medicine Program for Women (ELAM) (https://www.drexelmed.edu/Home/OtherPrograms/Ex ecutiveLeadershipinAcademicMedicine.aspx).

6. **Plant in soil already tilled**. Find out at which universities a national search for a chair has been completed within the past 6–12 months. Contact the Dean there and ask if she/he will share their short list with you. Was there a candidate they really wanted but could not hire because of constraints of funding, family, culture, or location?

7. **Who is 2nd in command?** The chair of the search committee can be advised to obtain the names of those individuals at top programs who are vice chair. The chair can request and review their CV and then, if indicated, proceed to contact the vice chair to probe their interest in the chair position.

Other considerations during the search process:

Alternatively, before creating a search committee, you may use this opportunity to meet with the entire faculty of the department and request that over the next 4 weeks, they organize a strategic thought exercise regarding the 5-year direction and needs of the department. They then are responsible for writing a "Leadership Statement" in which the characteristics and skills of the ideal new chair are enumerated. Once this document is complete, the dean can meet with the department faculty to decide on an internal vs. an external search and to set a timeline for completing the search.

If you are a Vice Chancellor/Dean, your responsibilities will include the hiring of the CEO of the hospital. In all likelihood, you have not been a member of administrative/business-specific leadership groups or societies, and hence, you may well need to involve a search firm. However, some of the above tactics may still be helpful, such as calling your fellow vice chancellors, especially those who have only recently completed a successful search for a CEO.

By becoming active, you will be able to **avoid the "Casablanca" conundrum** ("Major Strasser has been shot, round up the *usual suspects*." Captain Louis Renault – "Casablanca" 1942) and proceed to identify a truly unique pool of candidates from which you will be able to hire an individual who will be both congruous with your culture and simpatico with your vision for the school. The rewards here are most certainly proportionate to your personal expenditure of energy and oversight.

Search firms

The need to employ a search firm for candidate identification and recruitment was seen in various ways by the respondents: 27% always use a search firm, whereas 19% never use a search firm. The majority of the deans use them on an "as needed" basis. On average, by the time all is said and done, the average expense for involving a search firm is $250,000–$300,000. However, as one proponent of search firms noted: "Search firms add tremendous value, particularly in this era when academic faculty have much less time for deliberative and thorough seeking of candidates." Reasons for seeking a search firm include:

1. A failed search
2. Few candidates applying (e.g., seeking a chief information officer);
3. To increase the diversity of the candidates;
4. Internal lack of administrative support for the search;
5. Absence of competitive internal candidates;
6. The search is politically charged because of factions within the department.

On the flip side of this several-$100,000 coin, multiple deans expressed dismay at the cost of a search firm, their ancillary expenses for travel/lodging/meals, and the all too often disappointing results. Several deans weighed in on the less-than-sanguine aspects of hiring a search firm: "They charge an enormous amount of money, they always claim they can find candidates that no one else can, and you have to pay for their first-class airfare, hotel rooms, and then they charge you for every page they Xerox." "I rarely use search firms. When I have, I have been disappointed in their value." "I have used "big name firms" in the past, but I have tended to get a cookie-cutter type response, and they may bring us inappropriate candidates who do not fit with our culture."

In order to avoid this kind of outcome, the majority of deans using a search firm recommended vetting several firms before selecting one to use. In that regard, they relied strongly on recommendations from fellow deans and colleagues. *It is important to ask the search firm where they have placed an individual in the **same position** for which you are searching, so you can call the Dean at that institution and determine their level of satisfaction with the candidate hired and the conduct/cost of the search.*

Of note, among the deans, there was high praise for the small local firm.

These individuals more commonly made the effort to get to know the campus, its culture, and the dean's vision and thereby searched for candidates who would be a suitable fit. Indeed, one of these smaller firms actually guaranteed its work such that if the newly hired chair or center director failed to work out over the ensuing two years, the firm would repeat the search at no charge. Of note, the cost for a local firm where the recruiter you interview is indeed the same person who will do the search is far less expensive than a nationally known firm, often in the $50,000–$75,000 range.

Vetting the final candidate

"Hire well so you will not have to fire poorly." The hiring of a new chair or a center director is an opportunity for you to truly impact the culture of your institution. In this regard, there are several steps you can take to make sure the candidate is indeed the right fit.

1. **YOU make the calls!** (An absolute sine qua non) For the two to four finalists, you should *personally call SIX references for each one.* If they aren't listed already by the candidate, ask the candidate for the following individuals for you to call: two of their mentors or bosses, two of their peers/colleagues, and two of their trainees. Have a standardized set of questions that you can ask, and record the answers (Appendix VIII). With these six calls, you will learn a lot about the candidate that you would never be able to get from letters of recommendations or his/her interactions during the interview process. Some sources will tell you point blank that the person is not ready to be a chair and will back this up with chapter and verse; others will give a glowing review but also will be frank about shortcomings. Knowing an individual's shortcomings prior to their coming to campus provides you with an opportunity to provide a mentor, executive coach, or other tool to address the deficiency in an otherwise first rate hire. (N.B.: The search firm will tell you that you don't have to do this; all the more reason that *you DO HAVE TO DO THIS.*)

2. **Make more calls**: It is very helpful to *call the dean or chair at the institution at which the candidate worked prior to his or her present location.* As one dean noted, these individuals have no "hidden" agenda or aspirations for the candidate to leave, as might their current chair or dean. Also, it is helpful for you to speak directly with other individuals you personally know who are at the candidate's present or prior place of work. If the candidate objects to your calling

other individuals, you need to see this as a clear red flag. Although nobody gets along with everybody, more than one negative review should raise a caution flag. If the candidate raises the confidentiality flag to deter your calling, beware; defer but don't neglect to make the calls eventually.

3. ….**and more calls**: In making your phone calls, you might well consider contacting the office nurse or other subordinate (e.g., an administrative assistant) who has worked closely with the candidate. Again, you want as much information about this individual as possible; the more you know, the better the selection you will be able to make.

4. **Recruiting a surgical chair**: If recruiting a chair for one of your surgical departments, be sure to call the chief of anesthesiology, the chief operating room nurse, and one of the nurses who routinely scrubs with that surgeon. You will quickly learn about that individual's surgical abilities as well as their leadership and management style (e.g., temperament, punctuality, teaching abilities, grace under pressure, surgical skills, etc.). A key question in that regard is whether each of these individuals would have the candidate operate on themselves or one of their loved ones. Speech does not necessarily equate with one's manipulative abilities.

5. **Reverse site visit**: "Every time you get off your rear end (and) go to someone else's office you're sending the nonverbal message that they are very important." Should you as dean make a visit to the home institution of the candidate and visit her/his office, laboratory, clinical facilities, and operating room, or meet with his/her laboratory staff, nurses, current chair, or others? Half of the responding deans never do this, whereas the other half will do so on "rare" occasions (i.e., the recruitment is of major significance to the organization and entails the commitment of large amounts of resources). The cons for the reverse site visit are: expense to your institution, your time away, and the potential for making the finalist uncomfortable. On the flip side, the *reverse site visit manifests your seriousness/respect for the candidate while providing you with a clear view of the candidate's workplace* (i.e., how well is that individual "appreciated" in her/his own institution, what is the culture in which he or she is working [and is it similar to yours?], confirms the candidate's statements of accomplishment and effectiveness, and provides additional information on the candidate's

management style and personal characteristics).

6. **Final interviews**: To be sure, each candidate requires an interview with hospital leadership, the dean's office leadership, and key stakeholders (e.g., for a chair of neurosurgery, that would include the chair of neurology as well as the chair of orthopedics). There should be additional interviews with the specific department's faculty either in a group or individually depending on the department's size. It is to everyone's advantage to have the candidate visit with as many departmental faculty members as possible so a broad consensus can be developed in support of the candidate's hiring. Another interview to consider is to have the candidate visit with an executive coach with whom you are familiar and who knows your organization. This individual may supply information otherwise opaque to other members of the organization. Lastly, there is the "*hidden interview*" that occurs during the candidate's several visits to campus and that comes from the individual from your office assigned to squire the candidate through his/her day. This individual, who has repeated contact with all of the candidates, will have a unique view of each candidate, as the person will be able to observe/interact with the candidate as he/she moves from interview to interview, see how the individual responds to a stressful interview, listen to her/him handle phone calls in between interviews, and have a clear picture of their "nonshowtime" natural demeanor.

Negotiating the Chair's package

Developing the recruitment package for a chair is either a proactive or a reactive process. In the proactive approach, much preparation is required well before the search begins.

      a. A "blue ribbon" review of the department is performed, and the needs/goals of the department are determined. Alternatively, the department has gone through a strategic vision process and developed a plan that has been reviewed and approved by the Dean. *With either approach, a budget for identifiable department needs is created as part of the package.*

      b. In co-operation with the hospital leadership, a portfolio of resources is developed; this is based on a review of the department's past annual report to the dean and the departmentally prepared "strategic vision" document.

c. The search committee is made aware of the financial constraints so that it does not present candidates to the dean who are beyond the school's means.

d. The dean has a defined limit as to the size of the package and can make that known to the candidate if he/she so chooses.

In this manner, the chair package is fixed prior to the first candidate's visit. The leadership has determined the trajectory of the department based on blue ribbon recommendations and its own internal review of the department; how the department fits into the overall structure of the enterprise has likewise been set so it will best contribute to the strategic vision. The "heavy lifting" thus has been done prior to the initiation of the search. The new chair is hired to realize the well-defined vision of the leadership.

In contrast, in a reactive negotiation, it is the candidate who is asked to create his/her vision for the department (possibly including milestone achievements at years 1, 2, 3, 4, and 5). The resulting candidate's "ask letter" will make clear whether the candidate has done her/his due diligence in order to understand the needs of the department, and the institution's culture. It is helpful for the dean to provide the candidate with an outline for the construction of the ask letter:

> length (usually no more than 2–4 pages)
> divided into personal and departmental items
> subdivided into those items that the candidate feels are essential–*sine qua non* requests and those items that would be important but are not "make it or break it" requests.

Once this letter is in hand, the leadership proceeds to cost it out and prepare a business plan around the candidate's specific requests. The school may inform the candidate which items it will or will not be able to fund on a line item review. Alternatively, the cost of the requests can be summed and instead of accepting and denying requests one by one, the school's return offer may include a lump sum of funds to be invested in the department each year that can be used as the candidate sees fit to realize his/her vision. This strategy places the onus of balancing the budget on the new Chair and avoids numerous funding requests for other specific items that precipitously become "essential" after the new chair's arrival.

In some cases, a hybrid approach is taken in that the leadership has proactively reviewed the department and understands its needs, but still adapts a reactive approach to the negotiation. In this case, the response to the candidate's offer letter may be to add items to the package that the candidate has not considered followed by an in-depth value- and resource-based conversation.

Caveat

Avoid ever giving the candidate the sense that you are desperate to fill the position and that they are your only hope. This can be done by either negotiating with at least two candidates or more for the position simultaneously or, if down to one candidate, making sure she or he knows that you as dean are more than willing to repeat a search.

Repeating a search

"If you put the weak link in the chain, you only have yourself to blame each time it breaks."

The idea that a search has failed and needs to be repeated is one that plagues every dean. When a search fails, the dean needs to evaluate the search committee: Did the chair expend the proper amount of effort to identify candidates? Did the committee meet regularly? Was the search run well? Were the members of the committee committed to the process? If need be, replace the chair of the committee (noting in your records that he or she has failed) and change the committee membership. However, in the final analysis, the spin on this should not be one of failure but rather one of truly not settling for an inappropriate candidate and of emphasizing excellence over expediency. Indeed, a repeat search and a prolonged interim chair are far better than the expense and stress that will result from hiring the wrong person. The process may take a year or two. Remember, the candidate pool is not stagnant, and new individuals are constantly bubbling up.

10. DEVELOPMENT, EVALUATION, AND INCENTIVIZATION OF CHAIRS AND CENTER DIRECTORS

Development

The recruitment of a new chair is both time consuming and expensive. All too often, the endeavor ends with the arrival of the new chair, when indeed, that should be the beginning of a long-term mentoring relationship. To this end, there are multiple processes that can be brought to bear to develop and enhance the chances of successful leadership among chairs, center directors and the supporting leadership in the dean's office.

1. **Executive coaching:** The majority of respondents (55%) employ professional executive coaches at various times; for the most part, this is a reactive measure used on an "as needed" basis when a chair was failing. However, a few deans make executive coaching a proactive part of the recruitment package providing for executive coaching regardless during the initial year of a chair's tenure. This action shows a commitment to the success of the newly recruited chair while also ensuring that an executive coach who understands the school's culture and goals is working with the new chair toward her or his success.

   In today's environment, the executive coach serves a very special function in that he or she is the one individual to whom the Chair can truly unburden herself/himself and receive helpful feedback from an individual whose only interest is the chair's success. This kind of guidance cannot necessarily come from a more senior faculty member, as this is viewed as favoritism by the other faculty in the department. Likewise, it cannot come from a fellow chair, as all chairs are to some extent in competition with each other for limited resources. Similarly, it cannot come from the dean, given that most chairs are reluctant to bare their professional souls to the very individual who determines their employment and evaluates their performance.

The accomplished executive coach will more than earn his/her salary in saved recruitment costs. Although coach–chair confidentiality can never be breached, the coach can serve as a valuable adviser to the dean, informing him/her when an individual is simply "uncoachable," a clear sign that leadership change is needed or to alert the dean to a special need that, if satisfied, might preclude loss of a valued chair. The expense for this exercise is typically $25,000 for a complete evaluation (e.g., 360° evaluation, testing) and a 6-month engagement.

Caveat: If executive coaching is not part of the recruitment package and is offered after the chair's arrival, the chair will immediately assume there is an underlying problem. It is important, if indeed there is no underlying problem, to disabuse the individual of this notion. One way is to assure them that you are investing in their success, rather than trying to correct a deficiency. The executive coach will provide the client with a larger array of tools with which to deal with the challenges of being a chair. Another way is, if accurate, to share that you yourself employ an executive coach. In the final analysis, it is the rare individual who can self-analyze and redirect effectively; ongoing access to an unbiased domain-astute individual with their client's best interests at heart is an invaluable asset. By the same token, beware of the chair who repeatedly refuses the offer of an executive coaching experience; it is often a sign of a deeper underlying problem or a potentially flawed character (e.g., narcissism).

2. **Leadership courses**: A simpler, less expensive, method for developing leadership abilities among chairs is through leadership courses; two-thirds of the respondents offer this opportunity, although rarely is it mandated. These courses may be either external or internal. External courses usually are

through the AAMC or the Harvard training programs. Also noted to be of value in promoting female leadership development is the Executive Leadership in Academic Medicine (ELAM) Program for Women at Drexel University in Philadelphia.

However, a course will rarely create an "ah-ha" moment or accomplish a make-over. As one dean opined: "We depend on the chair's genome for success; i.e., intelligence, creativity, motivation, fire in the belly, leadership, and social skills (not linked genes!). None of these qualities is improved by courses." (Author's comment: However, the epigenome, when properly invoked, may modify some of the more noxious genetic products before they enter the general circulation.)

In addition to, or sometimes in lieu of, an external off campus course, many programs have developed internal campus leadership courses, often in collaboration with the university's business school. The scope of this endeavor differs greatly. This may be on a large scale, such as establishing an institute for professional development and leadership or a leadership academy. An organization of this nature has its own director and staff, who work with each chair to create departmental plans for faculty development and mentoring.

Alternatively, you may seek to create an internal leadership experience on a smaller scale. Working with either your own or a local business school, any of the following may be developed: single 1–2 day course, a formal leadership retreat, or the creation of certificate-granting modules (i.e., 6-week modules that include two full weekends plus 10–15 hours of night classes). The topics may cover human resources, conflict management, financial management, negotiation, strategic planning, etc.

If one elects to develop internal certificate-granting modules, these courses can be used as credits toward an executive or healthcare MBA. Of note, in a certificate-granting course, the student invariably needs to develop a specific project as part of the course work; this is an opportunity for the dean to assign a project to a chair such that it not only fulfills the course criteria but also serves double duty in addressing, and possibly solving, a decanal/departmental problem or need.

Other means of enhancing leadership among chairs, center directors, and associate deans may include a course on philanthropy (e.g., Advancement Resources www.advancementresources.org/Contact/Default.aspx) and/ or the 5-day or 2-day LEAN-Six Sigma program for improving efficiencies (e.g., Johns Hopkins University (leansigma@jhmi.edu or 410-637-7160). Projects beneficial to the medical school and hospital often emanate from these courses.

3. **Mentoring**: Lastly, and of great importance, is the mentoring that the dean provides through regular one-on-one meetings with the chair, during which problems are discussed and performance reviewed. Meetings of this nature should occur at least annually or preferably at least every 6 months; indeed, for some deans, these meetings occur quarterly or even monthly.

Evaluation

So you have hired a great chair, brought this individual onto campus, and have given him/her a wealth of resources. Now, how do you evaluate a chair's performance? There are two ways to serve this need: bespoke or store-bought.

To create a unique vehicle will take time and energy. The evaluation document needs to be on-line so it can be accessed and reviewed rapidly with the current data set against a backdrop of similar departmental information from past years as well as a contemporary dashboard of similar metrics in related departments (i.e., for the ENT dashboard, one might contrast it with the dashboard for orthopedics or urology). Although this is more time consuming to complete, it does provide a grouping of metrics that are specific to the execution of the school's strategic plan.

The contents of this "homemade" evaluation document are unique to each institution; the responding deans have provided a wealth of potential chair competencies (Appendix IX), which can be ranked from 1 to 5 (poor to excellent), with space provided for comments. Potential performance-defining metrics that the dean can track have been subdivided into the general areas of clinical care, administration, research, teaching, service (community and philanthropy) (CARTS) plus a sixth area, finances (Appendix X). In addition, to the foregoing, several deans have all chairs provide an annual performance evaluation of each other. Each chair is asked to rate each of their fellow chairs on her or his performance.

Alternatively, the dean can elect to purchase or adopt a ready-made chair evaluation template by using a specific agency's format for annual evaluations; these evaluations are computer based and housed in the cloud (e.g., Wiley Learning Institute's IDEA Center instrument at $295–$399/evaluation depending on if you wish to include training and development as part of the engagement or Faculty 180 from Northern Arizona University). A benefit of an industry-produced instrument is the opportunity to benchmark the performance of your chairs/center directors with their counterparts at peer or "better" institutions across the country.

Incentive program

So you hired a great chair, provided him/her with the resources to be successful, and he or she has delivered! Indeed, this person's ability is now widely respected across the campus and possibly nationally. Their stock has risen; are you going to incentivize the person to stay at your institution?

Slightly more than 70% of the respondents noted that they had developed a "bonus" incentive program for their chairs/center directors. A common method is to *set threshold, target, and stretch goals*, with the amount of bonus dollars dependent on a weighted goal-achievement process.

The funding may be done as a withholding of salary ($\leq 30\%$) or as a specified added dollar amount ($\leq$ $200,000) to be earned over and above one's salary. There are many variations on this model. In some places, no bonus is considered unless the department's financial performance is on target AND the chair has been judged to be a "good citizen," as evaluated by his/her fellow chairs; if these two aspects have been fulfilled, then the bonus incentives, which are school wide, rather than departmental, are activated. In one school, an individualized chair incentive plan is created as part of the offer letter (Appendix XI). In addition a set-aside of 200% of an incoming chair's salary is created to backfill for any portion of the salary that has not been earned over the initial 4-year period; in year 5, half of any remaining dollars in the set-aside are returned to the Chair for departmental development.

In contrast, almost 30% of schools have no monetary incentive plan. As one dean noted, rather than a defined bonus plan, they routinely reinvest in an *ad hoc* fashion in their high-performing chairs. This approach may be accompanied by nonmonetary awards such as recognition of the best performers in public forums, in the dean's newsletter, and/or in other school-wide communications. The downside of this approach is the potential for perceived favoritism, if the metrics for reward are not transparent.

11. RETENTION

You have struggled hard to create a culture, have developed a strategic plan to support it and have worked mightily to bring to campus a cadre of simpatico, energetic leaders to implement the strategic plan and grow the culture. The next challenge is how to retain these highly skilled individuals?

First, create a list of your *invaluable leadership members and chairs*. There will likely be key individuals in each realm of clinical service, administration, research, teaching, and community service (philanthropy). Determining your best leaders can easily be done by a simple 1-2 hour annual end-of-year exercise. Imagine if each of the leadership positions and each of the departmental chair positions in your organization were suddenly vacant. *Who among the current leaders and chairs would you rehire?* Alternatively or in addition, you may ask each chair or center director who they consider to be a true campus asset.

Once identified, these become the people, who need to know that they are indeed valued by you. Indeed, the best retention offer is the one that never has to be made because you have created an environment so enabling that your people are immune to outside recruitment offers. The only thing you cannot combat is if a leader/chair is going to leave for family reasons. Moving closer to home, especially if it is to care for ailing or aging parents, is a trump card, and when played, it is a clear indication that, regardless of your interests or the school's needs, the person is leaving. Accept it and begin the recruitment process.

Rumor, thought, visit, letter...at what point do you intervene to avoid loss of a valued chair or faculty member? How you first handle this situation becomes precedent...such that if you act early, you may be deluged by a variety of faculty seeking a "better deal," and if you act too late, the valued faculty member is already lost. The overwhelming consensus of the responding deans is to *intervene* early by meeting with the at-risk individual, before she or he even makes the first visit to a new school. The rationale for this approach is that you will have a better understanding of why the person is looking and have the opportunity to halt the process with a minimal expenditure of infrastructure and salary.

However, there is a minority opinion. Twenty per cent of the deans would wait until the candidate actually has an offer letter in hand and shares it with you. This approach is controversial and potentially inflammatory, and yet it sets a very clear policy and provides you with an idea of what the faculty member is being offered to move. It enables you to decide whether to walk away or make a credible counteroffer. It also enables you to know whether the offer is serious and whether the faculty member has an interest in staying at your school. Indeed, if she or he refuses to show you the offer letter (i.e., claiming confidentiality), you should consider calling the dean or department chair at the other institution. You may well be surprised to find out that the offer, as well as the letter, are fictitious. Indeed, at one institution, this tactic is carried to the extreme, whereby a counteroffer is made only if the offer letter provided to the dean is coming from an equal or better institution.

When fashioning a retention offer, it is reasonable to create a new appointment letter and have the faculty member co-sign it. Some deans would include, if the faculty is clinical, a non-compete clause; however, these are very difficult to defend. Another suggestion is to spread the retention package out over several years, which encourages the person to continue at your institution for several years and also avoids the problem of losing funds should the retention result in the faculty member leaving anyway, albeit a year later after the retention monies have been expended. Of note, 10% of deans include a sentence or two that the faculty member is also agreeing not to seek another retention offer for a minimum of 3–5 years. To be sure, the legality of such a clause, let along its enforceability, are uncertain. However, as one dean noted, "if they try this (i.e., looking for a position at another university) a second time, we congratulate them on their new job." Similarly another dean opined that any attempt at a second retention commonly fails, as clearly the faculty member has decided to leave.

12. TERMINATION

Rehabilitation?

"Firing of a chair is a personal failure of mine." It is in this spirit that a minority of the responding deans preferred an attempt at rehabilitation before proceeding to termination. At the outset, it is important to develop a timeline with a firm deadline of 4–6 months when a final decision will be made. During that time, a variety of interventions may be undertaken, either extramurally or within the confines of the campus. The former may include executive coaching with a 360° evaluation of the chair (noted to salvage as many as a third of troubled chairs according to 60% of the respondents), a leadership course (cited by 35% of the respondents), and/or an anger management program (noted by 25% of the deans). The executive coach can be of great benefit to both the chair and the dean. Indeed, after 6–8 weeks, a good executive coach will let the dean know whether further efforts will be fruitful or whether it is unlikely the individual will change. Leadership courses may be helpful; however, they are invariably more general than specific to the needs of the individual. The third option, an anger management course, is less commonly used, and typically the person vigorously resists or flat out refuses to attend. Indeed, great resistance is often a sign of poor self-awareness and pushes one more in the direction of expeditious termination. Other modes of intervention may include in-house human resources training, fiscal oversight coaching, personal counseling by the dean, meeting of the chair with his/her peers, or use of a facilitator to meet with the chair to seek resolution (one dean tried this on two occasions; it failed both times).

While pursuing a salvage intervention is a manifestation of hope and concern, the majority of deans were pessimistic about the benefit of any of the foregoing interventions, noting the expense and morale problems associated with delaying a likely inevitable conclusion. Indeed, several deans weighed in on this matter: "The tendency has been to "hope" that the individual will get better --- they often don't." "I think most people's personalities are well formed by their parents and genes long before they get to their job as chair, and I am, for the most part, underwhelmed by the ability of an outside intervention to reverse a downhill course." "Yes, we use these approaches. I generally do not find them to be effective." "I prefer to invest my money up front on leadership development with new chairs, feeling that chairs who are performing unsatisfactorily are unlikely to change their behavior." "When there is a lack of leadership execution, nothing ever really helps."

(A cautionary tale: *"the Don Quixote Syndrome"*: When you begin as Dean, you will often have this overwhelming desire to second guess the personnel decisions made by your predecessor. You may elect to bring back for a second look someone who has been cast off, believing that you have the ability to transform that individual into an effective, rehabilitated leader based on your subconscious desire to display to your faculty your commitment to them while simultaneously putting your mentorship abilities on display. *Don't fool yourself*–you likely will only expend a tremendous amount of energy and resources retracing the same painful path that your predecessor trod, only to complete the circuitous route and arrive at the same place he or she did months earlier.)

Termination

Terminations are likely the *most difficult and trying part* of being Dean. This explains why many deans have a tendency to procrastinate and to overthink the situation when, indeed, the trigger needs to be pulled sooner rather than later. As one dean noted: "In this case, the bird in the hand poops; better to go after the new ones in the bush."

Chair termination is most often the result of failure in one of four areas. Two of these are objective, data driven metrics: (1) *financial mismanagement* (e.g., insolvency, off budget, inability to heed financial guidance) and (2) *poor performance*. For clinical chairs, the key performance metrics would include work relative value units (RVUs), collections, student/resident teaching evaluations, philanthropic support, etc., whereas for research chairs, the key metrics would include peer review funding, publication record, teaching evaluations, etc.. The other two causes for termination are largely personality driven: (3) *loss of faculty support* (e.g., poor interpersonal relationships, poor peer review, lack of hospital support, poor leadership/mentorship, lack of vision, lethargy, faculty mistreatment, faculty vote of "no confidence") and (4) *cultural misfit* (i.e., unacceptable behavior). As one respondent noted: "You are hired for your skills; you are fired for your behavior." Behavioral problems include lack of integrity (specifically cited as the indication for termination by 20% of the deans), moral turpitude, disloyalty, lack of team play, poor communication, nonsupportive of the strategic plan, refusal to accept/embrace change, inability to act on advice, and refusal to recognize/support administrative goals. One or more of these factors was mentioned in each of the dean's replies.

Usually, the objective factors leading to termination are readily apparent to both parties. The subjective factors are more problematic, and termination solely on the basis of these criteria may lead to the chair filing a senate grievance or other "delay" rearguard tactic. Regardless, as dean, *you* need to do what's right as you see it and fulfill your duty to the campus rather than pander to the shortcomings of a single individual. Still, whenever termination becomes a senate or legal matter, the process becomes time-consuming and expensive, as the individual being fired often lacks the self-awareness to recognize their own shortcomings.

Given the lawsuit potential, prior to initiating termination proceedings, *almost all deans will engage their leadership group* in order to seek counsel as well as consensus. Commonly, the initial point of contact is with the senior associate deans/cabinet (cited by 50% of the respondents) or with the senior vice dean or executive vice dean or a trusted advisor. From there, if it is a clinical chair being terminated, the consultative circle may widen to include the hospital CEO with or without the other hospital leaders (i.e., CMO, COO) (55% of respondents). After obtaining a consensus to proceed with termination, some deans, albeit a minority of the respondents, would bring legal counsel into the loop to limit repercussions or other unforeseen consequences at the time termination proceedings are formally activated. If the decision is still in favor of termination, the concerns are brought to the attention of the provost, executive vice chancellor, president, or whoever else might be the dean's direct reports (specifically noted by 50% of the respondents). As one dean responded: "I always let my boss, the president, know of current performance issues so there are no surprises."

Once the nod from above has been given, additional people may be brought to the table: trusted faculty leaders/other chairs, trusted faculty from the affected department, board of trustees, and/or the faculty practice plan president. This initial groundwork pays dividends on the backend, as it may preclude senate or legal proceedings.

13. COMMUNICATION: SINE QUA NON

You can never communicate enough—in form or frequency. It is communication that often fills your life, be it with faculty, chairs, students, presidents, chancellors, donors, or staff. *Consistency, transparency and truthfulness* are the character traits that build credibility and trust. Those assets will see a dean through the worst moments that a school might experience. They are core values that must be hard-wired and never compromised.

The perception of you as dean is extremely important; you can no longer be seen as one of the boys/girls. The title of dean carries tremendous gravitas. As such, your ability to be spontaneous, humorous, and/or expansive in word or gesture, needs to be corralled; if 99 out of 100 people laugh at one of your jokes, the one person who found it offensive will become a matter of serious concern as a variety of services may be contacted, including but not limited to the campus ombudsman, legal counsel, and/or the office of equal opportunity and diversity.

Similarly, *choose your words carefully*. All of your responses are taken seriously and all too often what you said is either misquoted or not clearly understood; specifically any of the following utterances: "good idea", "interesting", "let's discuss further", "novel thought", morph into an imaginary affirmative "go ahead, two thumbs up" answer in the recipient's mind. Your subsequent failure to "deliver" on something you have no recollection of ever approving becomes a rapidly shared indication of your not delivering on "your promises"!

Meetings

The currency of most decanal communications is "the meeting." Meetings rapidly become the bane of one's existence. They can consume all waking hours, precluding any time for creative thought or visionary reflection. Managing meetings, both in number and in content, is essential for success and maintenance of sanity.

In essence there are three types of meetings: vertical: up (with your immediate supervisors/boss), horizontal (with your leadership team), and vertical: down (with your direct reports).

1. **Vertical-up**: A one-on-one meeting with your immediate supervisor (e.g., Vice Provost, Chancellor, President) for the majority of deans occurs every 1–2 weeks. Many deans remarked that they had a very close relationship with their direct report and commonly spoke with that individual more frequently than their scheduled one-on-one meeting. The responses very much indicated the importance of developing a collaborative and facilitating relationship, as this is the one person with whom credibility and trust need to be mutual.

2. **Horizontal**: (dean's office/leadership team): These meetings also differ in frequency, but most commonly, the dean and the key leaders in his/her office (i.e., dean's cabinet) meet weekly. Likewise, the dean may meet with the hospital CEO and or a small group of leaders from both the dean's office and the administrative offices for additional strategy sessions. These smaller weekly or biweekly meetings typically involve five or six individuals, all of whom are highly trusted, discreet, collaborative, and committed to the success of the institution.

3. **Vertical-down** (direct reports; e.g., chairs, center directors): These are meetings that the dean initiates or grants, and thus the dean would set the agenda and allot the time. In general, the agenda, is determined either solely within the dean's office or in concert with the key individual with whom the dean is meeting (e.g., department chair, chair of the council of clinical chairs). However, as one dean advised: never go into a meeting without first *knowing the agenda*. Not surprisingly, many of the deans noted that their meetings with chairs or center directors had a predetermined structured agenda. For example, an *established list of topics* under general headings was developed (e.g., budget, strategic planning, management issues, or review of previously agreed goals for the academic year) even to the point of subdividing the topics into chair's/committee's issues (addressed first) and dean's issues (addressed second). By proceeding in this manner, trust is engendered.

In general, the time allotted for a meeting is 15, 30, or 60 minutes; however, if you have a busy day, this may create a situation in which you are traveling from meeting to meeting with no time to decompress from the prior meeting before moving into the next. The day ends with you having multiple electronic or paper "notes to self" and upwards of an hour or more is needed to clear the decks. A solution is one dean's practice to schedule either 20 minute (on the half hour) or 40 minute (on the hour) meetings; this provides time to decompress, send emails related to the meeting, review your notes prior to the next meeting, and catch up on other emails or business, as there is always a 10- to 20-minute cushion between meetings. For this to work, you need a very attentive administrative assistant who will start your 20-minute meetings on the hour or half hour and then notify you by knocking on your door or calling your cell at 20 or 50 minutes after the hour; 40-minute meetings begin on the hour and end promptly at 40 minutes after the hour. Along these same lines, it is key for your assistant always to book travel time between meetings; one method of gaining some time between meetings is to a make sure the travel time is twice the actual time needed to get to the next meeting site. The goal is to finish the day unencumbered.

Meeting etiquette

Problematic in the meeting environment is managing the "electronic devices" in the room. At any given moment attendees might be on their cell phones, texting or on their hand held device/laptop computer batting away emails, tweeting, linking, face-booking, or gaming (as one dean noted, some faculty were playing an electronic game with other people in the room during the meeting). In this regard, several deans sought to limit the use of cell phones or computers during meetings. Indeed, when queried, many deans were supportive of an "electronics ban" during meetings, yet *only one dean had a policy forbidding their use.* The majority of deans preferred to rely on a common understanding that use of these devices during a meeting was rude and counterproductive. Indeed, as one dean observed, although people at a meeting were 100% physically present, they were only 80% mentally "there." Justification for this behavior came in the form of "Have them, use them. None of us has enough time." However, a more sobering stance was: "Meetings exist for people to talk to each other. People who are busy playing with their cell phones and laptops are not paying attention and *either the meeting is unnecessary for that person or that person is unnecessary for the meeting.*" As such, it is worthwhile considering who is essential at a given meeting and eliminating those who are not truly needed.

Dealing with the electronics problem may require, a private conversation with the offender(s). The other action is to have each meeting attendee surrender their electronic gear at the door to an administrative assistant, who can then answer any calls; this assistant can enter the meeting if indeed a particular call is urgent. Further, the dean can frankly discuss the matter with the leadership and chairs and thereby develop a mutually agreeable "electronics" meeting policy.

Similarly, when it comes to eschewing electronic device usage during meetings, the dean needs to lead by example. If you constantly have your computer screen or iPad between you and the people at the meeting, the consensus will be that this is acceptable etiquette, and the meeting attendees will do likewise; similarly, if you are taking phone calls during the meeting, others will follow suit. To obtain electronic "silence", you may consider having your IT department create one or two meeting rooms in which *internet and phone reception are blocked*; this will force everyone in the room to "listen up." One respondent noted that he/she routinely carries a notebook to each meeting and *takes handwritten notes*. This adds very little time and enables one to set an example and focus on the people in the room. After the meeting, an administrative assistant electronically scans the notes and sends them to the dean to download, review and file.

Meeting frequency

The overall consensus of the respondents was to hold one-on-one meetings with each chair *on a quarterly basis*. However, within the minority of responses, the breadth of established, regular one-on-one individual chair meetings ran the full gamut from "never" (as one dean replied: "Never. If I agreed to do one-on-one meetings with every department chair, Vice Dean, and Dean, I would not get any work done.") to monthly. One dean determined the frequency of department meetings according to the size of the department: hence, for medicine, surgery, and radiology, the meetings were every month, whereas for the smaller departments, the meeting with the chair was every 2–3 months.

An exception to the rule is for new chairs in which case, some of the deans would meet *monthly* with the new chair during her or his initial 2 years. Indeed, several deans frontloaded the first 2 months of a new chair's tenure with a weekly or biweekly one-on-one. This allows early discovery of any concerns (i.e., small problems, simple solutions) while providing an opportunity to mentor the new chair and immerse him/her in the school's culture.

In contrast to the one-on-one meetings, all deans met with the department chairs as a group usually on a monthly basis. In many cases, there were separate monthly meetings for the clinical and basic science chairs.

Aside from the aforementioned meetings, there are a host of other "mixed" meetings that may occur on a routine basis. A summary of the various meetings by title and frequency follows.

Monthly meetings

(1) **Dean's Leadership Council**: all chairs, center directors, hospital administrative leaders, and associate/vice deans.
(2) **Hospital and Medical School Finance Group**: dean, CEO, CFO of hospital, CFO of School of Medicine
(3) **Clinical Chairs** (possibly with clinical center directors): in some places, this meeting occurs every 2 weeks
(4) **Research Chairs and Research Center Directors**
(5) **Medical Executive Committee**
(6) **Practice Plan Executive Committee**
(7) **Government liaison**: updates on passed and pending legislation that impacts the medical center and school. Arrangements can be made during this meeting for visits with key state and national legislators, as well as with local mayors and other city officials.

One dean has adopted the practice of dedicating one afternoon a month to the aforedescribed Leadership Meetings. The following meetings all occur back to back on one day: Medical Executive, Council of Clinical Chairs, Council of Research Chairs, Physicians Practice Plan, and the Dean's Leadership Council. Accordingly, clinician leaders lose only a half day a month to these high level meetings. A broad expanse of significant issues is reviewed during that afternoon. The Dean's Leadership Council is the last meeting of the day; accordingly, individuals from the prior four leadership meetings are all together at the end of the day, allowing a more meaningful discussion and potential resolution of issues that may have arisen in the earlier, more focused meetings.

Quarterly – Semiannual Meetings: Town Hall Meeting

There was a common thread among the deans for conducting Town Hall meetings often together with the hospital CEO. The Town Hall meetings were usually scheduled every 3–6 months and were used to reinforce the mission/vision/goals of the school and as an open forum for frank discussion and feedback. To provide for the widest dissemination, the meeting often was podcasted.

Most commonly, Town Hall meetings were *general and open* to all faculty members, staff, and students. However, on some campuses, the Town Hall was stakeholder focused, such that there would be a series of separate meetings (e.g., medical students, full-time faculty, nursing staff or only members of the community). Another variation was to make the Town Hall meeting *topic oriented* (e.g., education, research, clinical affairs, finances, or professional development/advancement) drawing only stakeholders from that particular domain.

Annual meetings

(1) **Pan-departmental meeting** of the dean with a specific department's entire faculty: the dean presents an overall update of campus issues and progress and provides an open forum to address issues relevant to the faculty of that specific department. This is a perfect opportunity for a start/stop/continue exercise (i.e., what is the School of Medicine doing that it should stop doing? What is the School of Medicine not doing that it should start? What is the School of Medicine doing that should be continued?)

(2) **Chair's Departmental report to the Dean**: presented by the departmental chair to the dean, with all departmental faculty/residents/fellows/staff invited.

(3) **State of the School Address**: This address was provided by a *majority of the deans*; it was used as a tool to educate (i.e., mission/vision goals, update on education, research, clinical, financial, philanthropy, community, and strategic issues) and to expound on several "points of pride" in order to create among the attendees a sense of belonging to the university and to reinforce the school's culture.

Miscellaneous meetings

Among the respondents, there were a variety of other meetings albeit suggested by only one or a few of the respondents:

(1) **Faculty lunch** with the dean: monthly for 10 faculty on a first come, first served basis; open agenda

(2) **Student leadership lunch**: monthly with the leaders from each class

(3) **Chairs meeting**: every other week over a light dinner; no agenda

(4) **Executive committee of the faculty senate or full senate**: monthly or quarterly

(5) **Junior faculty meeting**: quarterly to discuss promotion expectations and issues

(6) **Dean's Lay Advisory Council**: quarterly. Of note, if one organizes an advisory council, it is important to make clear to

the members what their mission is: strategic (i.e., clinical, educational, research, and/or community outreach), philanthropic, or both.

(7) **Political community leaders**: annual. Includes the mayor, council members, state legislators, or national legislators, either in a general meeting or, more commonly, as a series of yearly one-on-one meetings.

(8) **Morning coffee in the doctors' lounge:** daily or weekly. One respondent makes it a ritual to visit the doctors' lounge *at a specific time each morning for 30 minutes* in order to foster informal faculty conversations.

(9) **Small group faculty meetings:** monthly. One dean invites 50 faculty *in alphabetical order* to a 1-hour session with the dean and the senior associate dean. Over the year, as many as 600 faculty are invited to a small group meeting with the dean and the senior associate dean. The attendee rate usually tracks at only 20%–30% of invitees, such that it is rare that more than 15 faculty members are present at any given session.

(10) **Dean's lunches:** monthly. In order to get a better feel for the campus pulse, one dean sets up 14 lunches over the year; only 10 faculty are invited at a time from among: *the top 20 clinicians* according to work RVUs, *the top 20 clinicians* according to collections, *the top 20 clinicians* ranked by "H" factor; *the top 20 researchers* based on NIH funding, *the top 20 researchers* based on total grant dollars; *the top 20 researchers* ranked by "H" factor, *and the top 20 educators* based on student evaluations/teaching awards. At these lunches, each attendee around the table is individually asked to participate in a *"Stop/Start/Continue" exercise* (i.e., what is the School of Medicine doing that it should stop doing? What is the School of Medicine not doing that it should start? What is the School of Medicine doing that should be continued?) These meetings identify major concerns, while also providing the dean with rare insights into "smaller" easily resolved problems.

Electronic communications: Bane and Benefit

No matter how computer illiterate you seek to remain, accept that the digital age is here, and you are most definitely a part of it. Better to embrace it rather than resist it, for the latter approach will cut you off from a majority of your faculty and from almost all of your medical students. The question is how to manage the various forms of electronic communications such that they do not consume you.

Email: The electronic storm

Email comes in four flavors for which different actions are appropriate:

(1) **Delete**: Another Amazon advertisement or the foreign prince who must divest himself of 10 million dollars and wants your help.

(2) **Acknowledge**: Notification of a request for a meeting or report that a task has been completed. For these emails, a simple one-word response should suffice (i.e., "perfect," "proceed," "good," "great," "yes," "thanks," "understood," a smiley face emoticon, or, when a toxic or noxious email has crossed your screen, "call-me"). This also saves the recipient time.

(3) **Act**: This email typically requires a several-sentence reply (e.g., arranging a meeting, exchange of information with your office administrator, social visit with a colleague/supporter).

(4) **File**: This type of email invariably needs some thought and a more lengthy reply (e.g., reviewing a manuscript, an assignment for you to write an editorial, request for a letter of recommendation). This type of email, after an initial brief response, can be "flagged" on your Outlook for additional thought either with a red flag, indicating you have not responded to the sender, or with a gray checkmark, if you responded but still need to do more work on it (left click on the flag box, and the red flag will appear. If you click a second time, the gray check mark will appear; if you want to remove the flag or check mark, right click and scroll down to "clear flag"). This way, the email remains on your screen as a reminder to complete the assignment. Alternatively, the last category can be printed out for further thought or added to your "task/to do" list so you don't lose sight of it. You can also work on your response as a "draft" (after left clicking on "reply," left click on "File" in the upper left hand corner of the top-most banner. On the second column of icons, left click on "move to folder," and then on the drop down menu, left click on "draft"). Working in "draft" mode is particularly beneficial if you are responding to a disturbing or sensitive email. Remember you don't have to respond to every email immediately: take the time to make sure your response is measured and thoughtful, and will "fly" when sent into the eye of the public.

Email is a *mosquito swarm*, buzzing incessantly (especially if you are using an audible alert), distracting, and occasionally leaving welts. Some deans retreat to the shelter of an administrative assistant who triages their email, thereby eliminating all nonessential messages. Your assistant can also unsubscribe you to all unsolicited newsletters. This works well; however, your constituents need to know that their email is being triaged. Other deans prefer to make it common knowledge that they are the only person who reads the emails sent to them, thereby assuring faculty that if they email the dean, the message remains confidential.

Email is the *Lernaean Hydra*. As you respond to one, two more take its place. To defend yourself, there are some important suggestions. First, *do not feel compelled to reply to each email* sent to you. Certainly, for those on which you are "copied," no reply is needed. As one dean's 96-year-old mother wisely opined: "You don't have to answer every question you are asked."

Email is a *one-way street*; you can't make a U turn. While you can request to "recall" an email, realize that it has already been sent and received and will appear in its original form in the recipient's inbox. There is one way to avoid sending ill-conceived emails or the all too common email that you send out referring to an "attachment" that you have failed to attach: that is to *work offline*. (If you are using Outlook, at the top banner row of icons, click the third tab, the "send/receive" icon; when it opens, in the second row of icons, go to the end of the row and left click on "work offline." At the right hand corner on the bottom of the page, there will now appear a white "x" on a red background and to the right of this symbol the words "working offline." Now, when you answer an email and hit "Send," your reply will go to your "outbox" but not be sent (listed vertically on the left hand side of the main Outlook page directly under "junk email"). After 10 replies, you can go into the "outbox" to review or edit any replies. This also allows you to attach the document you forgot to attach or to open and revise an email that may have been a bit too hastily written but felt so good to type ("you can then change words like "idiotic" to "ill-advised," "dumb" to "not wise," etc.). When you are ready to send your fleet of replies, go to the banner at the top of the screen and again click on "send/receive", then go to the end of the icons and then click on the "work offline" icon; you will now be connected to your email server, and all of the replies in your "outbox" will be automatically sent. Also, in the bottom right hand corner, you will now see either a yellow triangle with a red exclamation mark "trying to connect" or a yellow square alongside the word "connected to Microsoft Exchange.")

Email is a *sucker punch*. **Never** *open attachments from any sender you don't* *recognize*. By the same token, if you receive a strange email from a known source with an attachment but no message in the body of the email, don't open it. Instead, email or call that person to confirm its origin before you open the attachment. These phishing emails are getting more sophisticated so you may see them coming to you from Federal Express, a variety of banks, and "your" IT department. Once opened, any malware on the attachment will race through your computer. *When in doubt,* **don't open it***; call the information technology hotline or forward the email to them.*

Email has *weight*. One dean noted that he has related to faculty that the lengthier the email, the heavier it became, causing it to descend into the nether reaches of his "to-do/respond" list. Another dean noted: "I have had two chairs whom I told that I would read only six lines, so they'd better make sure what they want me to know is in those lines." It is amazing how some individuals have the time to compose a full page email without a single spelling error followed by additional lengthy emails despite your responding with a simple "thank you"; this is a problem and a phone call might be helpful but likely not. (Author's comment: I have fantasized, but not implemented, a plan to sum up the total number of emails and the total number of lines of email text received from each chair during the year. First prize for sending me the most number of lines would be termination, second prize would be mittens.)

Email is not *ping-pong*. If the volley of emails gets to three, consider a phone call to create a meeting on the topic or to end the discussion.

Email is not a *five alarm fire*. The consensus is that you should answer an email on the day it arrives. However if you answer every email immediately such that you are doing it on the elevator, while driving, or in the bathroom, people come to expect that you will always reply promptly, and thus, you have created a personal email Hades. If instead you can, carve out specific times in the morning and in the afternoon when you do email, then you will be in control and have the opportunity to fully focus on the various issues of the day without e-distraction. Also you will be surprised at how many emails answer themselves during the day and no longer require your input.

Alternatively, let people know your *hierarchy of availability*: cell phone, text, landline, email, or even a pager. In the case of an urgent situation, what mode of communication will insure their expeditiously getting in touch with you? In this case, you may elect to designate email as a form of nonurgent communication that you use to transmit information, create meetings, or provide praise. Yes, view all messages in your inbox on a daily basis; however, you may elect to wait until the weekend to clear your in-box.

Email is *open source*: Again, your response to email is **never** *confidential* regardless of how you mark the subject line (i.e., "for your eyes only," "CONFIDENTIAL," "attorney–client privilege") or the fact that you have sent it to only one person. Know that while something you receive may appear to have been sent only to you, you have no idea who or how many have been included via the "bcc" (blind carbon copy) on the email. All of your email should be viewed as though it were being *posted on a campus-wide billboard*. With that in mind:

(1) *Never respond in anger!*

(2) If you feel a pointed response is justified, see (1).

(3) If you just can't help yourself, dash off your uninhibited response in the fashion of Harry Truman. Let it all flow onto the page and then put it in the "draft" folder (vide supra, under **File**). Leave it in the draft file *for a minimum of 48 hours* and then reread and revise.

(4) Email is never humorous. Email is atonal, devoid of nuance, and has no body language … your great sense of humor does not play well within the confines of an email message. Resist the temptation. The spoken failed joke may become a ruinous lead balloon; the unappreciated "humorous" email goes viral.

(5) Nothing negative should ever be expressed in an email. *Praise should be written; criticism should be spoken.* No matter how right you believe yourself to be and no matter how right you are, a blistering or even mildly negative email or text will come back to haunt you, as your well-reasoned appropriate email will always be quoted out of context. As one dean noted: "always check each message before sending it to make sure your tone is civil and your spelling is correct."

(6) It is rarely appropriate to hit the "reply all" button. Urge others to similarly refrain.

Facebook, LinkedIn, Twitter

The rush of youth to social media (e.g., Facebook, Twitter, LinkedIn, Snapshot) with its 24/7 updating of each activity and it's sharing with everyone in your network and beyond has yet to be widely adopted at the decanal level. Although one-third of the deans were listed on LinkedIn, the majority noted that they never or rarely reviewed or posted on it. Further, only two deans were on Twitter, and one of them had sent only a single "tweet." Only one dean was on Facebook. However, three deans noted their creation of a dean's blog for posting announcements of new services, research awards, faculty news, and other positive events. As one respondent noted: "I have not found any negative consequences from my lack of personal involvement in social media. People who appear to need me seem to find me easily enough."

Texting

Despite its societal pervasiveness, the majority of the deans (60%) texted rarely and predominantly only for personal (i.e., family) matters. As one dean noted: "I don't want to give up being in the moment in meetings to answer texts." The counterpoint to this was the one third of deans who "texted" frequently; for them, the upside was that it provided a sense of immediacy, enabling them to respond to important events rapidly ("in minutes rather than hours"). One middle road approach is to have your IT department arrange your texting service so that only people listed among your contacts can text you. If you are clinically active, this precludes an incessant flow of patient- generated texts for which you are medico-legally accountable.

Voicemail

Nearly 3/4ths of the deans noted that they had an active voicemail account. Some noted that it was only on a personal line, to which only a few people had access. The minority of deans did not have voicemail, noting that they either "answer all of my calls" or just could not be bothered with yet another form of contact that would need to be checked regularly.

One broad recommendation is to *limit the number of ways in which people can contact you to three or four* (e.g., email, office phone, cell phone, text, etc.). Make your hierarchy of communication clear to all early in your tenure but remember that, if at the outset, you respond to each text or email immediately, you have set a precedent, and faculty will come to expect that as the norm. Bottom line, when it comes to communication *simplify your life*.

14. SOLVENCY: THE CURRENCY OF FREEDOM

Regardless of size, setting, or circumstance, the *sine qua non* for all schools of medicine is fiscal solvency. Getting there and staying there are two sides of the same coin. For a dean, *solvency is essential to longevity.*

Overall in approaching the finances of the School of Medicine, one has two levers (1) to *cut* (i.e., trim the fat) or (2) to *create* (i.e., to pursue new ways to enhance old revenue streams or develop new revenue streams ["blue oceans"]).

Cutting is by far the easier of the two and more commonly employed; however, the skill is to cut fat, not bone. The following is a list of cutting measures with respect to both *personnel* and *process* as suggested by the responding deans; of note, payroll far overshadows all other types of expenses.

Personnel costs

1. **Control/freeze hiring**: A first step to controlling this expense is to announce that for a period of time, all new proposed recruitments (i.e., anyone who would be on a School of Medicine payroll—faculty, nurses, administrative assistants, etc.) *will require prior review and signed approval by the dean's office.* Having the dean's office review all planned new administrative recruitments across the campus is a very effective cost-control tactic. Although this rule this may upset chairs and center directors, the potential for savings is large, as nonessential positions that become vacant are either not filled or delayed. Several deans noted that employment of a focused, committed, and well-referenced consultant is of great value in this regard.

2. **Consolidate or terminate departments**: To be sure, this is something to consider for a small department that has continued to run in the "red" year after year. There will be some expenditure of decanal political capital <u>among the members of the affected department</u>, but this will be offset by the message sent throughout campus with regard to how importantly you view departmental fiscal responsibility and how committed you are to righting the fiscal state of the campus. For example, a small poorly performing department of Physical Medicine and Rehabilitation can be reconfigured as a division within the department of Orthopedics, Neurology, or Neurosurgery. Alternatively, you can merge two related departments such as Family Medicine and a Department of Healthcare Policy and Research into one new department. Anticipated savings resulting from the combined services (i.e., shared administrators, residency coordinators, etc.) range from $400,000–$1,000,000 annually.

3. **Consolidate or terminate administrative positions**: Certainly, multiple departments in the basic sciences can often share a single employee such as a purchasing officer, chief administrative officer, or grants manager. In one school, the mandate was to cut 10% of the administrative positions in the dean's office and 10% of administrative positions within each of the departments. Savings in this regard are in the $500,000-plus range.

4. **Stabilize or reduce faculty salaries**: A salary freeze can be put into effect, but this will have an impact only down the line; the other option is to declare a 10% furlough. Before instituting salary reductions for clinical faculty, the first act is to establish a CARTS system (clinical/administrative/research/teaching/service) to track percent effort along with accurate tracking of each individual's clinical work RVUs. After this is completed, the next step is to create a clinical compensation committee (chaired by the head of the practice plan or the associate dean for clinical affairs) to review all faculty salaries and to align salary with work RVUs. As a rule of thumb, faculty at the 70th percentile of AAMC work RVUs for their rank and specialty generate sufficient collections to cover a salary at the 50th percentile of the AAMC pay scale. (Caveat: Don't assign yourself to this committee; you need to be the final arbiter of any disputes.)

For research faculty, salary is tied to research funding; for those who have lost funding, their salary can be reduced 10%–

20% annually for each year for which there is no salary support secured. Alternatively, if the school is in dire straits, a 10-15% furlough can be instituted. With this approach, the payroll declines immediately by 10%–15%. Usually, this is presented as a temporary (i.e. one year) emergency measure invoked to rapidly stop ongoing losses.

5. **No financial honeymoon**: Make it clear to all chair hires and to all current chairs that the physician hiring process has been streamlined, and *nobody* can be paid his or her salary until she or he is *fully licensed* to practice in your state and *credentialed* at your institution with all insurance plans. All new clinical hires should be seeing patients during their first week of employment. This simple measure saved more than $400,000 a year annually at a relatively small medical school.

6. **Buy-out program**: Consider providing a limited offer to buy out tenured faculty with a one-time payout of 200% of their salary. This can save $1,000,000 or more a year while opening up opportunities to hire less expensive, more productive non-tenured or tenure-track faculty. As one dean noted: "Faculty have historically interpreted (*sic* tenure) as a commitment to full salary for life irrespective of lack of external funding for (*sic* their) research."

7. **Alterations in retirement eligibility**: This can be done by *lengthening the time until a faculty vests or the time at the opposite end as to when one is eligible for retirement.* Potential savings of $2 million–$3 million/year. However, this tactic is contentious especially when applied to the time when one is eligible to retire.

Process costs—External

1. **Eliminate offices in leased building space**: Seek out empty or poorly utilized space on campus and fill it. You are already paying for that space, so use it well. Retire as much leased space as possible.

2. **Outsource**: Consider outsourcing the billing and collections office or your call center. This is at times dicey, as the devil you know may be better than the devil you don't; however, if the cost of the in-house unit is high, and the faculty satisfaction is low, outsourcing is a reasonable consideration. For instance, one can expect the cost of billing and collections with an outside agency to be in the 8% range, whereas the same services done internally often run at 10%–12%. On a $100

million book of business, each per cent reduction in billing costs is $1,000,000 of income added to the bottom line.

3. **Limit use of external consultants**: Too often, the response to a leadership vacancy is to hire a search firm to identify candidates, when indeed, for most clinical or research positions, relying on your outstanding faculty in that particular discipline to provide names of potential candidates is far less expensive and more effective. Also, as noted in Chapter 9, you as dean should be involved in developing the candidate pool. Similarly, when doing a strategic plan, you may have services on your campus through a business school that will provide the expertise you need at a very low price. Home-grown may do just fine and at far less expense.

4. **Debt relief**: Refinance the school's debt (e.g., consider getting a formal bond rating by going to Wall Street, which can lower the school's borrowing costs) or letters of credit on the deficit for major on-campus buildings. Savings accrue at $500,000+/year.

Process costs—Internal

1. **Departmental and center standardized budgeting process**: Create a standard template for entering each department's and center's budgeting process. Establish *hard deadlines for budget submission to the dean's office.* For departments or programs that miss their deadlines, consider taking them into receivership through the dean's office and managing their finances; this action will be a stimulus to all other departments to be timely and accurate in their budgeting. For the department that is in receivership, the dean's office has the opportunity to put into place processes whereby that department will become (and hopefully stay) solvent.

2. **Reduce hospital expenses**: Work with the hospital administration and the faculty to reduce hospital expenses. Standardizing operating supplies such as trocars, sutures, catheters, etc. can save hundreds of thousands of dollars annually. Consider introducing *LEAN training* and creating multiple cost-saving LEAN initiatives. Savings can be several million dollars/annually.

3. **Bulk Purchasing**: Standardize administrative and other office supplies across the medical center and medical campus.

4. **Malpractice cost reduction**: Review your current malpractice expenses or consider becoming self-insured; the latter can save upwards of $2 million–$3 million a year.

5. **Deactivate all purchasing cards**: This would include bank credit cards and the like; one dean noted savings of $1 million over a 6-month period.

6. **In-house capitated health plan**: Consider setting up an in-house capitated health plan in order to halt double-digit percentage increases in health insurance premiums.

7. **Workman's compensation**: Consider creating an in-house self-insured workman's compensation plan. Savings here are reportedly in the $3 million–$5 million range.

8. **Put the Brakes on your Information Technology (IT) unit**: Like a vacuum cleaner, IT sucks up a huge portion of any profits. The price tag for developing an electronic medical record often exceeds $100 million (some have hit close to $1 billion), and husbandry for the electronic behemoth commonly requires a $10 million plus annual outlay. This can break your budget faster than any other challenge. Beware of annual hardware upgrades at $2 million/year; do you really need them?

9. **Semi-annual expense review**: Review all expenses with your CFO every 6 months to see which are rising most rapidly requiring control and which can possibly be eliminated/reduced.

10. **Energy efficiency**: Use state of the art energy upgrades when renovating buildings or building new structures. Introduce energy-saving devices across your campus and develop an energy-saving culture by making your faculty aware of the cost of energy to the campus and how they personally can reduce that expense.

New revenue streams: Quick-Intermediate Term

1. **Revenue cycling**: The efficiency/effectiveness of your billing and collection unit is key to improving your cash flow. If you can't outsource it to the very best external unit, then the internal unit needs to be revamped such that it at least meets standard industry performance metrics. In that regard, the "report card" for assessing the unit's performance is rather simple, consisting of only five metrics: billing costs should be < 10% (ideally in the 8%–9% range), total number of days in accounts receivable should be < 75, net collection rate should

be at or above 95% (i.e., of the allowed, not the charged, amount for each insurer), claims denied should be < 5%, and claim lag from receipt of claim to posting should be under 5 days. An outside consultant (e.g. Huron Consulting Group Inc.) with hands-on capabilities can be very effective in improving your performance. Although expensive at first (i.e., upwards of $8 million–$10 million for the consultation that may last 6 months or more), the cost of the intense "boots on the ground" months long engagement will likely be returned within 2 years; the additional income to your bottom line in year 3 and thereafter may be $4 million/year or more such that your investment is recouped over a 4-5 year period.

2. **Maximize Medicaid payments**: As several deans noted, there are many potentially rewarding programs within Medicaid that often are overlooked. It is worthwhile to seek either in-house or consulting expertise in this regard. Three potentially beneficial measures include: utilize the "Upper Payment Limit Physician Reimbursement Program" (potential to increase reimbursements by $1 million or more, depending on your state program), work with the faculty practice plan to use intergovernmental transfers to support receipt of federal matching funds on Medicaid fee for service (potential positive add to the bottom line of $5 million–$7 million), and seek advice on how to maximize disproportionate share dollars.

3. **Hospital payments to the School of Medicine**: This is one place where a consultant (e.g., ECG Consulting) can be of great benefit. It is advisable for the medical center and the School of Medicine to *support this consultation equally*. The goal is for the hospital to pay a fair market rate for the various services it receives from the faculty of the School of Medicine. A complete unwinding of all services and an annual re-evaluation may add upwards of $5 million–$10 million to the bottom line.

4. **Strategic Opportunities Fund**: Work with the medical center to create an "incentive" formula, such that if the hospital exceeds a specified margin, has surpassed a predetermined number of days in cash, or has met its targeted decrease in overall per-patient costs, then a percent of that profit flows to the dean for the sole support of research and education. In this manner, the faculty can be incentivized to help with cost savings such as early patient discharges, purchase of all suture material from one vendor, and other projects beneficial to the hospital's bottom line. This approach

empowers the enactment of myriad LEAN exercises. This can bring millions of discretionary dollars into the dean's unrestricted fund while simultaneously providing encouragement to the faculty to "go the extra mile" on behalf of the hospital, knowing that some of the financial gain will be shared with the school of medicine and possibly with their department.

5. **New academic programs**: In particular the development of new *master's* programs can be beneficial (e.g., biomedical and translational sciences, marriage and family therapy, health professions education, systems biology clinical trials research, bioethics, bioinformatics, clinical research, physician's assistant program). However, this is not a big win, as even the most successful school with regard to creating new academic programs derived a maximum gain of $1.5 million/year. In general, the consensus was that new programs were "break-even" at best. As one dean noted: "No new programs generate revenue. All new programs just create costs." Similarly, community-based educational programs, such as a "mini-medical school" did not add dollars to the deans' coffers. In the same vein, the development of a post baccalaureate program was largely budget neutral or, rarely, mildly positive; however, a program of this nature is helpful in expanding a school's success with regard to diversity student recruitment efforts. Lastly, one dean noted a profitable school venture through the development of an international liaison for broadcasting simulation training for medical students from the United States to a foreign medical school; that endeavor provided nearly $300,000 of income.

6. **Tuition**: There are three ways you can approach tuition to improve your financial situation. One is the knee jerk reaction to *increase it*. This is always an unpopular move, and the gain in revenue is often counterbalanced by the goodwill lost among students and parents plus the possibility of freezing out potentially outstanding applicants. Still, for a medical school of 500 students, a $1,000 tuition increase will provide an extra half million dollars a year in perpetuity. Alternatively, one can seek a *bigger piece of the current tuition pie*; in other words, consider negotiating with the campus leadership such that more of the tuition dollars stay within the School of Medicine's budget rather than flowing to the main campus. The third option is to *keep tuition stable but increase the class size*, if you have the capacity without needing to hire additional faculty.

Along these lines, another tactic is if you are at a public medical school, you can *increase the number of out-of-state students* accepted into each class, as they will be paying a higher tuition rate. However, the benefit of this approach may be markedly blunted if your state constitution grants residency status after a year of in-state habitation. Among the responding public school deans, the goal for out of state students has been 20%–35% of the class; increasing this percentage further may engender a backlash from the state legislature.

7. **General campus support**: This is usually something that is best negotiated prior to your taking the position as Dean. On some campuses, funds flow directly from the Office of the Chancellor to the Dean's office for support of his/her initiatives. This may be in the $1 million–$2 million range.

8. **Indirects on research grants**: If indirects are not being credited to the School of Medicine budget, then *seek to increase the per cent of these funds flowing from campus back to the school.* The distribution of the indirect grant funds can be such that they are shared between the Dean's office and the department in the School of Medicine that generated the grant. It is recommended that the dean transfer all or a large percentage of the returned indirect funds to the investigator who generated the grant.

9. **Charging for services or facilities**: Although this measure often does not generate profits, it can enable the departments in which these services are provided to at least break even. Specifically, fees for IT, library utilization, teaching laboratories used for courses, or renting out a simulation center or clinical skills laboratory to other organizations (e.g., the fire or police department, emergency medicine technicians). Of note, a well-organized CME department can reach out to the community hospitals to offer their attendees CME credits; this extension of the service into the community can be the source of a reliable revenue stream.

10. **Dean's tax**: Increasing the dean's tax is a move that will raise howls from all faculty members even if the tax is already quite low (i.e. 5% or less). However, another way to increase income from the dean's tax is to move from a flat to a graduated dean's tax based on departmental collections. A graduated tax is fairer, more lucrative, and less disruptive. For instance, a flat tax of 4%, applied equally to the department of family medicine (annual collections of $2 million) and the department of neurosurgery (annual collections of $10 million)

would generate $480,000 in annual revenue to the dean's office. In contrast, a graduated tax that ranged from a low of 3% to a high of 5% would have family medicine pay only 3%, or $60,000, on its $2 million collections, whereas neurosurgery, at 5%, would pay $500,000 on its $10 million dollar book of business, for a total return to the Dean's office of $560,000 in taxes, a 16% increase in revenue. To be sure, the surgical subspecialties such as neurosurgery, ENT, orthopedics, and urology have a much higher earning ability than family medicine, pediatrics, and internal medicine; the dean's tax should reflect these differences.

Additional support dollars can be accrued by making sure that the dean's tax applies to *all* clinical income; this includes income from clinical procedures as well as from the net gain derived from sale of devices (e.g., eyeglasses, orthotics). Furthermore, in some schools, the dean's tax applies to many types of nonuniversity faculty income, including honoraria, legal payments from being an expert witness, and industry consulting dollars.

New revenue streams: Long Term

1. **Government**: Get involved on a local, regional, and state-wide basis with your representatives and legislators. It is important for the dean to educate government officials/representatives as to the school's challenges and its contributions to the community. It may be worthwhile to consider hiring a full-time individual whose only job is to serve as a government liaison; this individual is responsible for creating decanal visits with government individuals as well as alerting the dean to *new legislation* that may be beneficial/threatening to the School of Medicine. One dean noted that a lobbying effort resulted in a state-supported ($2 million) cancer research initiative; this in turn drew the attention of a donor, who further supported the endeavor with a $10 million gift.

2. **Develop an entrepreneurial culture**: Certainly, drug and device development can generate significant cash flow from shared royalties or licensing agreements. At a few schools, the derived annual cash flow is in the tens of millions of dollars. The key is how to foster a culture of marketable discovery. Three suggestions were: (1) for the Dean's office to hire an Associate Dean for Industry Relations. This is a person with an

MBA and an entrepreneurial track record who can serve as an effective liaison between faculty and industry; (2) encourage industry to partner with the university by relaxing rules on intellectual property (e.g., the University of Wisconsin and Penn State have done this most effectively); and (3) consider setting aside research space on your campus that start-ups or more established companies can rent at a low rate provided they are engaged in product development or testing with one of your faculty. With regard to (2), it would behoove you to take a hard look at your technology transfer office and evaluate their 2-, 5-, and 10-year performance. You may be surprised to learn that the cost of the office exceeds the return from licensed or sold intellectual property and thus consider downsizing the technology transfer unit.

3. **Increase research support**: This can be achieved in many ways: traditional NIH grants, grants from industry partnerships, new research enterprises that draw community support through philanthropy, and development of a robust clinical trials program.

4. **Community hospital support**: One dean noted that hospitals in the community provided additional support to the School of Medicine; this amounted to nearly $40 million a year.

5. **Innovative contracting**: One school reached out to the public health sector and offered their services to several state agencies. This resulted in funds flow for direct patient care (e.g., providing healthcare for prisoners) and for consulting services (e.g., disability evaluation reviews, workman's compensation issues, payment for care of dual eligibles).

6. **Philanthropy**: This is so important that it has its own chapter (Chapter 18). Philanthropy can be transformational as more and more medical schools are being named for the $200 million plus donor. Smaller gifts lead to support for new buildings, unrestricted funds for the dean's use, and the creation of endowments for faculty and laboratories. The lofty goal of endowing every medical student slot has yet to be realized by any of the established schools; the best situation occurred at one school that noted that their endowment covered 50% of the educational expense. Various appeals to donors include: naming of the School of Medicine (this is in the hundreds of millions of dollars and has occurred at both UCLA and Mount Sinai with the Geffen and Icahn Schools, respectively); naming a building (usually in the $15 million–$30 million range); developing a tuition relief/scholarship fund,

challenging each alumni class to endow one student tuition; and the development of a friend/fund raising annual medical school gala (proceeds usually in the $1 million range). Specifically, one dean noted they do their alumni weekends in 5-year intervals for each class; hence, at any given time, students at the alumni weekend may be celebrating a 5, 10, 15, 20, 25, etc. year reunion. Each reunion class has its scholarship fundraising leader with the goal of eventually raising sufficient funds to endow a medical student tuition in perpetuity (roughly $1.5 million) or provide $40,000–$60,000 to pay a year's tuition for one student.

In the final analysis, it is essential to develop a *culture of fiscal accountability and responsibility*. This will require the clear message to the leaders of all departments and centers that all budgets need to be complete and submitted to the office of the dean by a specific date (usually 4 months prior to the fiscal year close). Furthermore, before any budget is reviewed, you can mandate that the department have a dean-approved faculty incentive plan. Lastly, the chairs and center directors need to know that *accuracy in budgeting* is a metric by which they will be evaluated. The teeth in all of this is that the *dean's office reserves the right to take any department into receivership* if it is off budget by more than 10% for more than one quarter. (Paradoxically, this may include departments that are under budget by more than 10%, as this is indicative of a poor budgeting process in that department; sadly, some departmental chairs seek to hide assets by "low-balling" their budget. Once in receivership, this practice can be corrected.) In receivership, *all departmental expenditures are under control of the dean's financial team* until the department is back on budget. Although this may seem overly onerous, it does work, and indeed, departments classically running in the red manage to maintain fiscal solvency after coming out of receivership.

Table 2. Seeking Solvency

		I. Cutting costs			II. Creating income
Personnel			Quick intermediate fix		
	1.	*Freeze hiring*		1.	Revenue cycling (5 metrics)
	2.	*Consolidate/ terminate departments*		2.	Maximize Medicaid payments
	3.	*Consolidate/ terminate administrative positions*		3.	Review hospital support to the School of Medicine
	4.	*Stabilize/ reduce/ furlough faculty salaries*		4.	Create a hospital based strategic opportunity fund to support education and research
	5.	*No pay on your first day unless you are fully licensed and clinically active*		5.	Start new academic programs (i.e. masters programs)
	6.	*Buy out tenured faculty*		6.	Tuition increase
	7.	*Reduce retirement benefits either in amount or timing (time to vest/ retirement date)*		7.	Increase support from general campus by obtaining or increasing return of part of medical students' tuition paid to "campus"
Process costs				8.	Increase return of indirects
(external)	*1.*	*Eliminate leased space*		9.	Charge for all services or use of specialized research facilities or CME credits
	2.	*Outsource*		10.	Move from a flat to a graduated dean's tax / increase dean's tax
	3.	*Limit outside consultants*			
	4.	*Debt relief through refinancing*	Long-term	1.	Seek legislation supportive to the

						School of Medicine
(internal)	1.	*Standardize budgeting process*		2.		Entrepreneurial culture
	2.	*Cut hospital expenses (e.g. bulk purchasing of hospital supplies, AM discharges, Lean programs to eliminate waste.)*		3.		Increase research support (especially through clinical trials)
	3.	*Cut administrative/office expenses (e.g. bulk purchasing)*		4.		Community hospital support of the School of Medicine
	4.	*Renegotiate malpractice costs or become self-insured*		5.		Innovative contracting for services (e.g. workmen's compensation, etc.)
	5.	*Deactivate all purchasing cards*		6.		Philanthropy
	6.	*In-house capitated health plan for all employees*				
	7.	*In-house workman's compensation program*				
	8.	*Scrutinize and reduce the IT budget*				
	9.	*Quarterly expense review – identify rising expenses and seek ways to decrease them*				
	10.	*Energy efficiency cost savings when renovating or building*				

15. RESEARCH: SUSTAINABILITY

"Research loses money." How, then, in times of waning support can research programs grow and thrive? There was no "ah ha" reply in any of the returned questionnaires. As one dean lamented, "this is a work in progress, yet to be achieved."

Sadly, the once robust standard peer review national funding sources are no longer sufficient to sustain today's American scientist. To wit, each new or renewed NIH grant is a bittersweet occasion, as the dollars provided by the grant are *insufficient* to accomplish the proposed studies since the "approved" research budget is rarely equal to the "submitted" research budget. Furthermore, not only the scientist but the institution itself is challenged, as the dollars provided to support the university's research infrastructure (i.e., the indirect expenses) similarly fall short (*vide infra*). As such, each new NIH "success," although prestigious, further drains funds from the dean's office.

When queried on ways to overcome the ever-widening gap in research support, the most common reply was for more *philanthropy*! (See Chapter 18). Researchers need to understand the importance of being able to articulate their research in lay terms. To this end, investing in a course on philanthropy specific to the research community may be of benefit. Organizations such as "Advancement Resources" can provide a yearlong course of 4-hour quarterly dinner meetings on philanthropy along with a set of meaningful attendee deliverables (i.e., faculty homework). Alternatively, advancement at your university can organize these instructional courses. Subsequent recommended activities may then include intimate dinners bringing a few donors and a passionate researcher together and/or high-quality lay research seminars designed to bring the donor public into direct contact with your philanthropically astute scientists. The expense of any of these activities is rapidly recouped as soon as one researcher succeeds in securing even a modest gift.

Four other external sources for potential research funding are foundations, industry, local or state government support, and non-NIH federal funding. However, tapping into each of these sources requires an investment in additional personnel.

1. **Foundation grants**: Approaching *foundations* (e.g., Gates, UniHealth, Keck) is sufficiently time consuming to justify *hiring one advancement* person whose sole job is to research, visit and apply to foundations within a 100-mile radius of your school as well as study those foundations that may be simpatico with your mission, albeit physically more distant. Visits should be arranged so you can be introduced to the foundation's executives and present those areas of your school's mission that would be aligned with the mission of the specific foundation. Visits of this nature ought to occur as often as every 3 months.

2. **Industry grants**: Garnering *industry support* can be mutually beneficial; however, it is to your advantage to develop a uniform approach to industry and work with your technology transfer office to overcome the usual self-inflicted wound of overvaluing and overcomplicating access to your school's intellectual property. As one dean noted, royalty and licensing agreements usually are *insufficient to sustain a robust technology transfer program*. Although some programs derive annual incomes in excess of $5 million, this is the exception. Indeed, both Penn State and the University of Wisconsin have largely walked away from their IP, allowing them to save funds by downsizing their technology transfer office while simultaneously becoming more friendly to industry.

   Also, the development of biotechnology start-up facilities/incubators on your campus can be very helpful. These centers of innovation require a large infusion of funds to initiate but have the potential to generate large returns; still, this is noted to be a high-stakes gamble. A simpler and less expensive way to initiate an incubator effort is to start small; one can create an innovation "garage" by repurposing any unused laboratory space and renting it to industry with the proviso that there must be a faculty member working with that industry on a given project. These "tech-portal" endeavors provide some income to support the research infrastructure, encourage faculty to work with industry, and may be the source of worthwhile royalties or licensing agreements down the road. In this regard, the hiring of an *Associate Dean for Corporate*

Relations is a worthwhile endeavor, provided the person occupying that position has a MBA and a track record of entrepreneurship so he/she can serve as an effective university–industry nexus. In addition, this individual will have the time to visit with your faculty and encourage/facilitate their entrepreneurial interests.

3. **State and local government grants**: Additional potential funding opportunities are available from *state and local government*. As with philanthropy, foundation work, and industry relations, this endeavor will require expanding your infrastructure and hiring a full-time dedicated employee. Lobbying specific government representatives for research dollars in an area that has touched their lives can be highly productive. If your university is in the same city as the state capitol, there is an even better opportunity to get to know your state government officials and to lobby for research support. Two deans noted that they were successful in obtaining a one-time state-designated budgetary line item for $10 million or more, one for cancer research and another for the study of neurodegenerative disease. In California, the state-budgeted California Institute for Regenerative Medicine has been a huge source of support for stem cell research, as have funds derived from the state's tobacco settlements.

4. **Other (non-NIH) granting agencies**: Lastly, on a national and regional level, there are a host of *non-NIH federal funding opportunities*: Department of Defense, Defense Advanced Research Projects Agency (DARPA), Veterans' Administration, and the recently established Patient-Centered Outcomes Research Institute (PCORI). Again, mining these opportunities requires a dedicated person.

To address the aforedescribed funding opportunities, one dean created an Office of Strategic Initiatives for seeking state and non-NIH federal funds. Ideally, an office of this nature would have four individuals, each with a specific focus to raise funds from foundations, industry, state and local government, and non-NIH federal organizations.

At an internal level, research funds can be derived from two sources: the *dean's tax* and a *hospital pass-through*. School of Medicine taxes on clinical revenue range from 5%–10%. As previously noted, it is important to define "taxable" clinical revenue and decide whether this applies only to professional fees or to all income derived from clinical practice, which would include departmental compensation from sideline businesses (e.g., sale of weight loss supplements, eyeglasses, skin care products, etc.). Similarly, a decision needs to be made on whether all outside faculty income (e.g., honoraria, fees from doing legal work, consulting, etc.) is taxable. Third, it is helpful to consider a graduated rather than flat tax, as the former provides substantially more income. However, as several deans noted, although this is income to the dean's office, it is also "robbing Peter to pay Paul," as each of these departmentally-focused tactics negatively impacts the departmental budgets and thus creates a zero sum game for the School of Medicine's budget.

Hospital support for research and education remains a hard sell, especially in the face of today's waning hospital reimbursement and increased hospital expenses (e.g., the electronic medical record, regulatory expenses, etc.). One strategy is to link research to quality improvement projects in which the hospital has a vested interest and thus may provide funding for specific projects. Specifically, researchers in health policy and epidemiology may find this to be a fruitful source of funding. Another avenue is to develop in concert with the hospital CEO (and the Chancellor's support) a *strategic opportunity funds flow model* such that if the hospital hits specific targets (i.e., margin $\geq$ 5%, days in cash > 70, or decreasing expense per patient), then on a formulaic basis, funds will flow to the dean's office specifically earmarked to support research.

Finally, the dean can be creative in trying to foster innovative and collaborative research endeavors among the faculty. The old saw of "you need to spend money to make money" applies, both with regard to expanding the advancement staff within the School of Medicine, as previously noted, and in selectively investing, incentivizing, or otherwise stimulating the scientific community to "rescue" itself. The responding deans had several suggestions in this regard.

1. **Presubmission grant review committee**: Junior faculty should not be forced to reinvent the wheel when it comes to applying for NIH or other peer reviewed funding. Capitalize on your "homegrown" talent by creating a NIH *pre-review grant committee* comprised of faculty members who have served on an NIH grant review section. Mandate that no new grants from assistant professors or first-time applicants will be submitted without first being reviewed by this committee 6 weeks prior to the submission date. Although participation on the committee can be viewed as service, better results may be obtained with even a small payment for the reviewer's time; this can be divided such that a certain amount (usually a couple of hundred dollars) is given to the senior scientist for doing the review, and an equal amount is set aside as a reward for that same individual should the grant get funded. In the long run, this approach saves funds, as poorly done grants are not

submitted to your contracts and grants office, thereby lessening their workload while enhancing the chances that the grants that are submitted will be favorably reviewed.

2. **Internal funding**: The dean can create a *lottery* whereby one or two unfunded grants that were within 10% of the pay line are randomly selected for a year's worth of internal funding with the proviso that reapplication will occur the following year.

3. **Bridge funding**: *Bridge funding* needs to be available for researchers who have been highly productive but are (optimistically) in between grants. A formal policy in this regard needs to be established so the amount of funds available (usually around $50,000/year) and the indications under which they are made available are clear. For example, you may create a policy whereby for every 4 years of peer-reviewed funding, a year of bridge funding is "credited" (i.e. banked) to the investigator to be used when needed.

Lastly, it is important to bring together researchers of similar interests in order to stimulate collaborative and highly creative endeavors. In this regard there were many suggestions:

1. **Interschool dinners**: Invite faculty from the School of Medicine to dine with faculty from another school on campus (e.g., Engineering, Biological Sciences, Law, Arts). These dinners can be limited to 25 faculty members from the School of Medicine and 25 from the invited school on a first-come, first-served basis. Both deans attend the dinner to kick it off. At the dinner, attendees are asked to *sit next to someone they do not know*. During the dinner, each attendee is asked to deliver to the group a *1-minute overview* of their research interests. Prior to dessert, the attendees are encouraged to move and sit next to someone whose interests are similar to their own. These dinners are best done as a pair; one dinner is on the medical school campus, and the second is on the campus of the visiting school. At 3 months, a follow-up questionnaire may be sent to all participants to gauge the development of any new initiatives.

2. **Topic-directed dinners**: A pancampus invitation goes to all faculty throughout the university to attend a dinner that is *focused on a given topic* (e.g., vision, hearing, 3D printing, stem cells, stroke, brain injury, nanotechnology, simulation in education, etc.). The dinner is limited to 25 individuals

from the School of Medicine and 25 from the general campus on a "first-come, first-served" basis until all 50 slots are filled. The format of the dinner and follow-up are identical to the aforedescribed interschool dinners.

3. **Triumvirate grants**: A call for grants goes out that requires *three* principal investigators from different departments/schools (e.g., a clinical department in the School of Medicine, a basic science department in the School of Medicine, and another school on campus such as Engineering, Biological Sciences, Law, Humanities, etc.) or one PI from the School of Medicine and two PIs from different campus schools). For this activity, $80,000 needs to be set aside, with the first prize being $50,000 and a second and third prize of $15,000 each. These grants can be reviewed by an external committee (e.g., at another university) or by a group led by the Senior Associate Dean for Research. Subsequent peer-reviewed grants submitted by the awardees and successful new funding are tracked as a metric for the program.

4. **New programs**: New programs can boost grant funding or even generate funds to subsidize other, less lucrative but equally important research endeavors. One campus established a *new academic department* called "Quantitative Health Sciences." This new department recruited individuals from six fields: epidemiology, biostatistics, health informatics, outcomes assessment, health services research, and health disparities research. The outcome was $50 million in new awards over a 5-year period. The deans also noted that creating a new center of discovery encourages cross-campus collaborative efforts and may facilitate the recruitment of well-funded researchers. The following is a list of *new scientific disciplines and clinical research foci* that were either absorbed into a department or used to form a new department or center of discovery at various medical schools:

   a. **Disciplines**: Systems (or integrative) biology, computational biology, bioinformatics, stem cell studies, epigenetics and metabolomics, drug discovery, genomics, gene therapy, RNA therapeutics, vaccine research, molecular biology, molecular structure, lung biology, population health, and nanotechnology.

   b. **Clinical research areas**: Autism and behavioral neuroscience, neurodegenerative diseases, traumatic brain injury, infectious diseases, cancer, behavioral health, imaging research, comprehensive alcohol research center, cardiovascular research, personalized medicine, regenerative medicine, comparative effectiveness and health outcomes research.

A potpourri of other measures to support or streamline research include:

1. **Match funding to space**: First, it is essential to determine the total square feet of research space on your medical school campus and then to record how much space is dedicated to each investigator. Once this is known, the total grant support to that investigator needs to be recorded, such that one can calculate the *dollars of support/square foot of research space*. This can be done on a running 3-year average and may be set at a different threshold for assistant, associate, and full professors. It is encouraged that this endeavor be by consensus (i.e. through the office of the Senior Associate Dean for Research in concert with the Chairs of the basic science departments) rather than executive fiat if at all possible. However, once the funding per square foot of research space falls below a specified level, the laboratory space is reduced accordingly. It is essential that the faculty understand the policy and that the policy be uniformly applied and enforced. In this manner, you will be able to support and develop your strongest, best performing faculty while culling less productive members from your midst.

2. **Efficiencies**: Scrutinize your entire research infrastructure, including the offices that preside over grants and contracts, investigational review board (IRB), clinical trials, and technology transfer. Are there efficiencies that can be introduced to decrease costs while improving grant flow-through? This is ideal for a LEAN project.

3. **Establish a 501c (3) Medical Science Foundation**: This entity is established as an external, *stand-alone facility* with loose university ties. Its mission is to support the School of Medicine's research mission. This type of entity may be very appealing to donors.

4. **Research Strategic Plan**: While many schools have an overarching strategic plan, one may consider a separate endeavor to establish an aligned research strategic plan. One dean attributed a near doubling in NIH-supported research

centers to the implementation of a research-specific strategic plan.

5. **Return of indirect funds**: Whenever there is a financial crisis, a common hue and cry from the research faculty is that 100% of the indirect funds from their NIH grants should be returned to the investigator. The fact that dollars need to be expended to maintain the buildings in which the research occurs seems to be a foreign concept to many faculty; indeed, at many institutions the indirect funds fail to cover the basic infrastructure costs, as other research dollars (e.g., donor or industry) may come with little or no funds for infrastructure support. As such, at many universities, the cumulative indirect income falls to half of the real cost of maintaining the research facilities. It is not surprising that the return of indirect grant funds from the campus to the School of Medicine ranges from none to little (the average return noted by the deans was in the 10%–15% range). The one exception (and indeed, there was only one response like this) occurs when the School of Medicine is responsible for the indirect expenses of its own research facilities; then, 100% of the indirect funds become the property of the School of Medicine and the dean is saddled with the responsibility of finding ways to subsidize the shortfall. Regardless of the schedule used, it is of the utmost importance that the distribution of indirect funds *be uniform* and *transparent to all faculty* or else the cacophony over indirect funds is unending.

6. **Share**: Create a catalogue/directory of all research equipment on your campus that costs more than $10,000. This on-line listing should include the laboratory in which the piece of equipment resides, the lead researcher, and what the "recharge" rate is for using the instrument. Regardless of how any piece of equipment came onto the campus, *all instrumentation needs to be available to all researchers*. The "recharge" dollars may be used to pay for the service contract of the particular instrument, placed in a savings account for the purchase of a new machine as the current one is depreciated, or shared with the investigator whose grant allowed purchase of the machine. In this manner, you can avoid the duplication of expensive machinery on your campus while ensuring that what you have is used effectively and efficiently.

On a personal level, the majority of deans have not been able to continue their own research efforts. Although some were able to do so at the beginning of their term, most were unable to sustain their laboratory beyond a few years.   A few deans noted that they were able to keep a "hand in" the laboratory by transferring their research responsibilities to their on campus collaborators.

16. EDUCATION: MAINTAINING ACCREDITATION AND EDUCATING FOR EXCELLENCE

A common theme among the deans was that the educational process continues to grow in both complexity and cost. The following chapter covers accreditation, curricular change, classroom reform, digital technology, introduction of medical ethics and medical humanities into the student curriculum, dean–student interaction, and lastly, fiscal challenges.

Accreditation and the "visit" from the Liaison Committee on Medical Education (LCME)

Nothing will catch your attention more than the build-up to an LCME visit. This is an independent body that is equally supported by both the American Association of Medical Colleges (AAMC) and the American Medical Association (AMA); here is where everything is on the line. If your school fails the site visit and is placed on probation or worse, losses accreditation, the repercussions reverberate for years to come: poor student recruitment, loss of faculty, and likely the loss of your position as dean.

When do you start preparing for a LCME site visit? *NOW!* Regardless of when the visit is scheduled you should always be looking to be prepared for the next LCME site visit. Indeed, 20% of the responding deans noted that at their school, LCME site visit preparation is *a continuing quality improvement project* resulting in an ongoing state of readiness. Dashboards addressing all aspects of a LCME visit are developed and updated monthly or quarterly. *One administrative full-time employee is assigned to this project.* The completeness of the dashboard and progress in each area is reviewed routinely by the Senior Associate Dean for Education; the dashboard results are reported quarterly to the Dean and at the dean's cabinet meeting.

The first steps toward a successful LCME site visit is for the Dean to emphasize to the leadership how important an exemplary site visit is to the School of Medicine and to the Dean personally. In this regard, you should be very much a part of *reviewing the preliminary self-study documents*, both for the school and from the students. Indeed, to gain additional knowledge of the process, you may volunteer to accompany an LCME site visit to another institution or volunteer to become a member of the LCME. In addition, at the annual AAMC meetings, it is prudent for you and/or your Senior Associate Dean for Education to attend all of the sessions pertaining to LCME site visits, as the requirements for accreditation are frequently updated.

It is not feasible for you alone to lead the charge, given all of your responsibilities; you need to develop the personnel who in turn will inform the processes necessary to make the site visit a success. Regarding personnel, it is key to have *one person whose sole responsibility is the LCME site visit and the updating of the relevant metrics*. This can be the Senior Associate Dean for Education or an individual with prior LCME experience whose time can be purchased to provide this service. This is the person who will organize the LCME committees, make sure that all aspects of the report are properly assigned, ensure that the *self-study document* is progressing according to the timeline, engage the department chairs, provide materials to educate all staff and faculty on LCME standards, incentivize the students (along with the Associate Dean of Student Affairs) to complete their part of the self-study survey, organize a mock LCME visit, attend accreditation sessions at the AAMC meetings as well as LCME workshops, edit the school's final *self-study document* (i.e., the Data Collection Instrument [DCI]), and report on progress or lack thereof to the dean at each cabinet meeting. If you don't have such a person on your staff, now is the time to hire one.

Among the deans, there was also consensus with regard to doing a mock site visit 1–2 years prior to the official site visit. Some places elect to do this internally, but most of the respondents recommended *an outside reviewer*, specifically, a person who had been a site visitor, a prior member of the LCME secretariat, or a consultant. If you have a 2-year lead time, you may be able to correct any identified deficiencies.

Several other helpful ideas are:

1. **Educate staff and faculty on LCME standards**: This can be done by creating a website 2 years prior to the LCME visit. The website can also serve to aid the

completion of the *self-study document* by increasing faculty and student engagement in the process.

2. **Track the monthly "Connecting with the Secretariat"**: that is produced by the LCME and is on their website.

3. **Create an in-house electronic LCME dashboard**: that can be used to provide quarterly updates of activities such that when the visit is near, *all pertinent data* can be assembled easily.

4. **Outside consultant**: If you are already on LCME probation, hire an *outside consultant* to provide the bandwidth and knowledge that you need in order to rebuild and move off of probation.

5. **A caveat**: *Never start a new program in the reporting year!*

Curriculum

The backbone of every medical school is its curriculum and yet while presented as fully cast, it is more like an eternal cartilage that is continually being reshaped rather than being allowed to ossify. Indeed, the degree of curricular change introduced by the responding deans over the 5-plus years of their tenure was extensive. To wit, the traditional department-based medical school curriculum was *abandoned at 90% of the schools*. Among the remaining 10%, all but one, at the time of the questionnaire, was involved with moving toward a system-based curriculum. However, this is not at all surprising, given the mandate of the LCME since 2000 to move away from department-based curricula. As one dean noted: "In 2002, the LCME told us: "What part of managing your curriculum centrally didn't you understand? Fix it or go on probation."

An organ-based and/or system-based curriculum is overwhelmingly employed during the initial two years of medical school. This has led to a marked reduction in standard didactic lectures (e.g., on average, only17% of a student's time is spent in lecture) and to a significant uptick in small group learning along with the attendant need for increasing the number of clinician educators. This has also resulted in the inclusion of clinical experiences during the classically basic science first two years of medical school: (1) clinical ambulatory experiences with primary care physicians; (2) week-long clinical intensive exposures (e.g., shadowing experiences); and (3) widespread use of standardized patients.

Another type of broad curricular remodeling that had been introduced at several schools was *problem-based* or *case-based learning*. In this curriculum, there is little to no time spent in didactics; instead, there are clinical scenarios at the core of small group sessions, team training, small group simulations, and other limited group and individual learner-centered activities. The goal with these programs is to facilitate the translation of knowledge into effective action. The price to activate this kind of curriculum is further expansion of the teaching faculty and/or an increase in the amount of teaching time per faculty member.

Several novel curricular concepts were espoused by the responding deans. One such concept was the creation of *pathways* to enrich student learning in a highly focused area. For example, in an "urban health" pathway, students are provided clinical experiences in an urban setting as well as becoming involved in research projects focused on health delivery in an inner-city environment. Another novel concept is the creation of a *two-tier system* in which students may elect to follow a classical 4-year education or a "specialty track" curriculum. In the latter arrangement, students are simultaneously accepted into medical school *and* into the residency program in their discipline of choice at the same institution. Their curriculum is modified according to their chosen future area of specialization, thereby reducing the time spent in medical school by almost a year. A third program altered the curriculum based on the social interactions of the students. The basis of this plan is the creation of *learning* communities, each consisting of 12 students. The group stays together over the entire four years of medical school and maintains the same physician mentor; they see patients in the ambulatory clinic together throughout their 4 years and do their internal medicine clerkship together.

Many deans emphasized the importance of ongoing curricular review. This may take the form of an *annual or semi-annual half-day retreat*. During the retreat, the content and performance of the curriculum are reviewed. Alternatively, this can be an outgrowth of a more formal *strategic planning exercise in medical education*. The result of this more expensive and time consuming endeavor is the creation of a 5-year roadmap to curricular reform and a successful LCME site visit. An exercise of this magnitude needs to include all stakeholders: department chairs, outstanding faculty teachers, student leaders, and alumni.

As the curriculum evolves and societal demands for physician services increase, there is a push toward developing *competency-based curricula* that rest on a solid foundation of computer and digital technology for teaching and evaluation. This raises a recurring question regarding chronology vs. competence as the criterion for graduation. Whereas the former is the "tried and true" approach, advances in technology make the latter an attractive and possibly a more cost effective alternative for ensuring a capable physician work force. However, as of 2016, none of the responding deans had introduced a competency-based curriculum that would allow for a variation in the time to graduate.

Classroom Reform

There is an educational Catch-22 at many medical schools. The students don't want to come to class because the class is poorly taught, outdated, or irrelevant; the teachers teach poorly because nobody comes to class, and hence classroom work is viewed as a less-than-a-worthwhile expenditure of faculty time. The Dean or Senior Associate Dean for Education needs to step forward and take control of the situation. Various corrective actions were suggested:

1. **Student attendance**: Create an 80% **mandatory attendance** policy. Attendance can be tracked via personalized clickers or tablet technology (e.g., a specific question is asked and answered during class such that an individual's attendance is logged). This can be started only with the incoming class provided they have been informed that this is the school's new policy. For students already at the school, adherence to the policy can only be encouraged.

2. **Faculty evaluation**: Make sure that teachers understand that going forward, each of their *lectures will be evaluated by the students*. At the end of the lecture, a few minutes is reserved for student evaluation: a variety of factors are provided that need to be "graded" on a scale of 1 (poor) to 5 (outstanding). These evaluations are reviewed by the Senior Associate Dean for Education; teachers scoring ≤ 3 need to be *remediated or terminated*.

3. **In class faculty evaluator**: Consider hiring an interested faculty member to "go to medical school" and over 2 years, attend (or listen by Podcast) to all of the first- and second-year lectures and critique them. This individual's evaluations can aid in enabling poor lecturers to improve as well as defining needed change.

4. **The privilege of teaching**: Create within your school's culture the clear understanding that *"teaching is a privilege"* and should be valued accordingly. Annual bonuses and honors may be distributed to the best teachers; the latter should be presented in a very public forum.

5. **Incentives**: Reward those departments with the highest teaching evaluations and let chairs know that departmental excellence in teaching is an important part of their annual evaluation.

6. **Listen**: Create an annual lunch opportunity (usually two lunches) with your top 30 educators based on medical student ratings or student teaching awards. The dean can use the lunch

as a stop/start/continue exercise (*vide supra*: Chapter 13: Communication under "Miscellaneous Meetings" [10] page 64) to gain further insight into the teaching mission.

7. **Academy for Excellent Teaching**: Creating an honorary teaching organization (e.g., Academy for Innovation in Medical Education). Entry into the academy is reserved for the school's best teachers and maintenance of membership would require completion of education-based projects beneficial to the school and its students. The Academy would be responsible for creating faculty learning sessions with regard to digital teaching enhancements such as a tablet curriculum, podcasts, simulation exercises, flipped classrooms, etc. The Academy typically needs to be funded through the dean's office; however, it is money well spent, as it provides recognition and education for the top teachers and encourages myriad improvements in the educational process. The Academy members can also be of great help during preparation for the LCME visit.

8. **Innovative courses**: Consider introducing innovative courses such as an introduction to Lean 6 Sigma, care of the hospitalized adult, perioperative care, or quality, safety, and process improvement.

9. **New student programs**: Develop innovative student programs such as student wellness, career counseling, or a student success committee charged with evaluating key factors resulting in student success in medical school. The last can include efforts to identify struggling students and provide mentoring/tutoring.

10. **Seek counsel**: Consult with the dean (or suitable member) of a local School of Education (e.g. Dept. of Instructional Design), which can be very helpful with regard to developing an academy (vide supra [7]) as well as evaluating, selecting, and implementing new educational technologies for the medical school curriculum.

Digital Technology

The 21st Century has installed computing technology firmly into the learning process: podcasts, flipped classrooms, simulation mannequins, as well as tablet computing. This revolution in the delivery of information has ushered in the age of *personalized learning* ("...the ability to tailor information delivery to students according to their learning styles."). Today's learning occurs in a solitary or small group environment; teachers, rather than spending class time lecturing, instead directly interact with the class to create an understanding of the assigned material thereby empowering the student to effectively apply the new knowledge to case studies and clinical scenarios.

The entry of these educational enhancements into the medical school environment is pervasive. As one dean noted, consistent with multiple replies: the use of technology is "...*absolutely essential* for new millennial learners." Classes are now awash in tablet computers (80%), podcasts, on-line lectures, small group learning experiences, flipped classrooms (60%) (i.e., class time formerly used for didactic purposes is now used for interactive discussions designed to enforce the use of newly acquired knowledge), and simulation exercises (65%) through highly sophisticated programmable computer-based mannequins or standardized patients. Rather than memorizing vast tracts of text, the success of the millennial student is judged by her or his ability "*to leverage digital technologies to curate, analyze, and incorporate the best medical knowledge into practice.*" Lest we lose the old, amidst the new, one dean warned "...do not give up letting students touch patients and look them in the eye. They are not going to have practices of mannequins."

It is sobering to realize that the biggest impediment to these changes is not the learner, but the teacher. Poor classroom preparation or persistence in presenting the "same old, same old" lecture pushes students to avoid attending class and to seek information from a more palatable, updated platform via the Internet. As multiple deans noted, if teachers are to remain relevant, they must *become computer literate* and adopt/adapt the new digital technology to engage their students. This will require more effort on the part of the teacher than heretofore was needed to "teach a class."

To aid teachers in crossing the "digital divide," many deans have turned to an existing or newly created *academy for medical education (vide supra*: Classroom Reform [7]). Within the academy, lectures and workshops are provided on how to create a podcast, flip a classroom, develop simulation exercises, etc. Alternatively, some medical schools have expanded the medical education faculty to include a director of simulation as well as a director of instructional technologies and additional assistant staff in order to develop the various simulation scenarios, properly program a clinical series of events into the computerized mannequins, facilitate faculty in creation of their podcasts, purchase electronic medical texts, and upload materials to the medical school's website. In addition, many schools are now introducing point-of-care ultrasonography into their curriculum to further expand the value of performing a traditional physical examination. A couple of schools also have begun studies on the use of Google Glass in which the glasses are worn by the standardized patient, thereby providing the teacher with a very clear "view" of the student's bedside manner as seen through the eyes of the patient.

Medical Ethics

Despite being the presumed bedrock of the medical profession, medical ethics to some extent, and medical humanities to a large extent, remain *outside of the mainstream curriculum* of most medical schools. Like the soil from which a bountiful crop grows, neither is appreciated as being essential to the final product until well after the harvest (i.e. graduation).

Nearly all respondents noted the importance of medical ethics and noted its presence in their curriculum. By far the most common modality for teaching medical ethics was to make it *part of a "thread"* moving through all 4 years (40% of schools) or at least the last 3 years (25% of schools) of medical school. The "thread" took on many configurations: case discussions in core clerkships, dedicated topic-oriented seminars, or a required written paper on an ethical issue (e.g., end-of-life care, ethics of practice, resource utilization). In 20% of schools, medical ethics was appended to a more wide-ranging course (e.g.: "Patients, Physicians, and Society," "Ethics, Humanities, and Professionalism," "Physicianship"). However, a required defined course specifically devoted to medical ethics was cited in fewer than 15% of the responses; the course was most commonly entitled Clinical Bioethics and was given in the latter half of the second year just prior to the start of the clinical rotations. The total time devoted to teaching medical ethics over the 4 years of medical school *did not exceed 60 hours* at any school.

Medical Humanities

Medical humanities broadly encompasses "… an interdisciplinary field of humanities (literature, philosophy, ethics, history, and religion), social science (anthropology, cultural studies, psychology, sociology), and the arts (literature, theater, film, and visual arts) and their application to medical education and practice. The humanities and arts *provide insight into the human condition*, suffering, personhood, our responsibility to each other, and offer a historical perspective on medical practice." The question regarding the inclusion of medical humanities in the curriculum drew many divergent answers, ranging from consternation (e.g., "I am not sure what qualifies as medical humanities") to high-level recognition in the form of an established Department of Medical Humanities (two schools).

The teaching of the medical humanities was *absent from nearly one third* of the schools. Among those schools with a program in medical humanities, the majority had either a separate course (e.g., "Doctoring, Medicine, and Behavior" or "Patient Spirituality") (Appendix XII) or introduced the medical humanities as part of the teaching of medical ethics. In a third of the schools, electives were offered in the medical humanities;

the subject of medicine was intertwined with a broad range of topics: literature, law, music, film, history, science, philosophy or war.

Dean–Student Interactions

To be sure, there are never sufficient hours in the day to minister to all the needs of a medical school's constituency and the intricacies of its growth and finances. Thus finding the time to engage each class of students in a meaningful manner is an ongoing decanal challenge. Although practically all deans surveyed attend student orientation, match day, the White Coat ceremony, and commencement, these are relatively impersonal exposures, as the officiating duties are invariably podium bound. Some deans also make it a habit to attend the first lecture of the year to the first- and second-year students. Also, if your school has created "learning" communities (e.g., dividing the class up into five or six communities, each with no more than 25 students and a "faculty" house leader), the Dean can visit each of the communities once or twice a year for a "dine and discuss" session.

In response to the question how to foster better student communication and interaction, **four opportunities** were most commonly cited: *dining, teaching, interactive events,* and *student leadership.* Far and away the most common interface between the dean and a group of students is through dining. Usually, this occurs in groups of 8–15 students and may be over breakfast, a late afternoon snack, lunch, or dinner. One dean invites students selected at random from each of the four classes to lunch. Other deans seek to interact with all members of each class each year, by inviting students to lunch in groups of 15 until all students have at least been extended an invitation. At the lunches, a stop/start/continue conversation (*vide supra*: Chapter 13: Communication under "Miscellaneous Meetings" [10] page 64) may be initiated with each student. Notes from the students' responses can be shared at a MedEd meeting or directly with the Senior Associate Dean for Education.

Heightened student interaction through **teaching** takes several forms. For some deans, this may be an annual lecture(s) to a given class, whereas other deans conduct an entire course (e.g., history of medicine or medical ethics). In other cases, a more personal encounter is provided by a dean's clinical office practice through which students may rotate. Also, some deans tutor specific students during the school year in their particular discipline. One dean goes on a medical mission to a third-world nation each year with a small group of students.

On a broader scale, whole class informal **interactive events** were highlighted by several respondents. This may take the form of an annual get together at the Dean's home. Depending on the class size, several parties may need to be scheduled in order to bring all members of the class into direct contact with the Dean and his/her spouse. This is most commonly done for the incoming freshman class and may be scheduled for the Sunday prior to orientation. Other informal gatherings cited by the deans included an ice cream social for all members of the second-year class, an annual Dean's sponsored student party (often on Match Day), a student body 2.5-day retreat, an annual holiday party, a "happy hour" (medical and graduate students), or a winter/spring dance. For the hardier, a student athletic event may be planned, such as an annual softball game/picnic or a faculty–student doubles tennis tournament with each team consisting of one faculty member and one student, or a 5K "fun" run/luncheon (not luncheon/run!).

Alternatively, the Dean may schedule medical student class-year-specific town hall meetings (with pizza) on an annual, semi-annual, quarterly, or, more rarely, monthly, basis. The town hall can be either a formal agenda-laden or a more relaxed, conversational event; in the latter circumstance, an alumni friend(s) may be invited to attend. In some cases these meetings are topic oriented (e.g., sports medicine, advances in medical technology, career opportunities in the military, etc.) and paired with a knowledgeable faculty member(s) or lay person(s) in order to provide the students with an opportunity to broaden their potential occupational horizons. These activities are meant to promote comradery among class members as well as introduce students to the Dean.

At an individual level, some Deans have set aside an hour a week for student office hours; individual students can schedule a 15-minute appointment. Other one-on-one activities with students may occur during the Dean's clinical office hours (e.g., "shadowing" experience) or in the Dean's laboratory. At one school, a sterling silver baby cup is given to any medical student who has a child while in medical school; a ceremony is held to honor or bless the child, and the cup is given to the new parent(s) by the dean and his wife.

The **student leadership/government** plays an important role in the School of Medicine, which is further legitimized by the Dean's involvement. Meeting with the student leaders allows the dean to take the vital signs of the student body; this approach was undertaken by only one third of the respondents. Meetings with the student body leaders usually took the form of a lunch meeting, which occurred monthly, quarterly, or semi-annually. In one case, the Dean attended the student government meeting and provided an update of the school's legislative, research, teaching, and clinical programs, the content of which was identical to similar presentations to board members and to the faculty; in this way, the dean sought to create an atmosphere of consistency, transparency, and credibility. Another opportunity is to meet with the student representatives to the American Medical Association.

Fiscal challenges

Fiscal solvency of the medical education enterprise has become more difficult given the increasing call for costly digital technology to enhance and evaluate student performance. In addition to the four previously described fundraising tactics (*vide supra*: Chapter 14) of increasing student tuition, expanding class size, a graduated departmental tax, and education-earmarked philanthropy, there are *three other education-specific potential levers* to pull:

1. **Foundation support**: This may come in the form of *scholarships* (e.g. UniHealth) or *programmatic support* (e.g., Macy Foundation). Staff in the medical education office need to be encouraged/incentivized to apply for grants of this nature.

2. **Federal funds**: These funds may come through HRSA. One school secured federal funds to support the development of a 5-year program for educating physicians for a career in urban health.

3. **Student fundraising**: The medical school class may elect to develop funds for specific endeavors (e.g., student clinic, cancer prevention such as "Movember" for prostate cancer, an endowment in memory of a departed student). This may take the form of an annual student chili cook-off day, student involvement in the annual School of Medicine gala, or even a dance marathon. However, given the huge amount of knowledge that today's medical students need to amass and the small amount of funds these endeavors actually raise (usually less than $10,000), there is concern about the wisdom of diverting students' attention from their studies.

(Author's note: Amidst the press of clinical and research demands/costs, medical education may unbalance a school by becoming the short leg of a three-legged stool. To prevent such an occurrence, one might view the medical education administration as though it were a center or department, with the Senior Associate Dean of Education functioning as its director/chair. The Senior Associate Dean thereby becomes *responsible for all aspects of the educational process* from quality of lectures to fiscal solvency, just as the chair of any of the clinical or research departments would be. It is also this person's responsibility, in consultation with the Dean, to prune the medical education office of ineffective personnel and to oversee the curriculum and eliminate poor teachers. Faculty in the Center/Department for Medical Education would include the assistant education deans (e.g., basic sciences, clinical, simulation, graduate medical education) as well as the most active teaching faculty from each department.)

17. CLINICAL CHALLENGES

Today, every vice chancellor/dean of a School of Medicine is faced with **three daunting clinical challenges**: (1) clinical *alignment* with the medical center/hospital; (2) development of a *viable methodology* to ensure funds flow from the medical center in support of the mission of the School of Medicine; and (3) *clinical funds enhancement*. Each of these areas becomes vastly simplified if there is a Vice Chancellor of Health who presides over both the medical center and the School of Medicine. The following paragraphs presume that a more traditional arrangement is in place in which the CEO of the hospital and the Dean of the School of Medicine *work together* to meet the clinical challenges.

Clinical alignment

Clinical alignment is a natural outflow of an institution's *culture*; without the right culture, no amount of strategic planning or consultant engagements will provide the desired alignment. The culture of your institution is mutually defined by you, as the Dean, and the CEO of the medical center. Both individuals need to be passionately in agreement as to the mission, vision, values, and goals of the institution. Specifically, the CEO, coming from a business background, needs to be educated as to the culture and needs of the research and education mission, while the Dean, coming from a medical academic background, needs to become educated about the standards of the corporate/finance world. *Mutually agreeable goals* need to be clearly determined at the start of each academic year. Accordingly, it is key for the dean to envision and explain educational and research goals in business terms defining them as projects, for each of which the following are elucidated: *objective outcomes, milestones, timelines, deliverables,* and *performance evaluation*. To this end, the two individuals need to trust each other and develop a mutual respect for one another. If this is not the case, then it is time for a change in leadership.

Clinical alignment requires integration between the hospital and the School of Medicine, which most commonly takes the form of a mutually developed *strategic plan (vide supra:* Chapter 7). Also, it is important for the CEO and Dean, along with their respective leadership teams, to serve together on a variety of committees. This can occur through membership in the clinical operations committee, enterprise committees, etc. The frequency of these meetings may be biweekly or monthly. In addition, in the spirit of transparency, the CEO should have a member of the Dean's leadership committee in his/her cabinet meetings, and similarly, the Dean should have a member of the CEO's leadership group (e.g., Chief Strategy Officer) in his/her leadership cabinet meeting. Integration also includes *joint recruitment* by the Dean and CEO of clinical chairs as well as of the medical center's leadership (e.g., Chief Medical Officer, Chief Financial Officer, Chief Strategy Officer, Chief Operating Officer, Chief of Information Technology, etc.). The key is for both the Dean and the CEO to identify individuals to bring into the organization who will be enthusiastic "joiners" rather than passive "followers". *Finally, it is very helpful for the Dean and CEO to meet one-on-one every one to two weeks.*

Integration can be furthered by the creation of a Clinical Enterprise Executive Leadership Board that is *advisory to the CEO and Dean.* Members of this committee include the head of the faculty practice plan, the president of the council of clinical chairs, key hospital leaders (i.e., COO, CSO, CMO, CFO), key medical school leaders (CFO, Associate Dean for Administration, Senior Associate Dean for Education), along with one chair from each of the three major disciplines: hospital services (i.e., Anesthesiology, Pathology, Emergency Room, or Radiology), surgery (e.g., general surgery, neurosurgery, orthopedics, etc.), and medicine (e.g., internal medicine, family medicine, neurology, psychiatry) . In the case of the board reporting to a Vice Chancellor of Health, the board would also include the Vice Dean and the CEO. This board would meet for 2 hours weekly, biweekly, or monthly; it serves as the nerve center for the combined medical school and medical center campuses and is responsible for reviewing all new clinical business proposals.

Funds flow

The flow of dollars from the medical center to the medical school is the life blood of the latter. As one dean noted, it is essential to convince the hospital to "invest in the clinical and academic enterprises of the medical school. This requires an enormous amount of work, communication, and listening." However, as one EVC and university

President noted: "If we didn't have a medical school, we wouldn't have a hospital…we are in the education business, not the hospital business." This kind of support from the central administration is *invaluable* in bringing the hospital to the table in order to develop an equitable funds flow model. Unfortunately, given the current impact of the electronic medical record on hospital expenses, the introduction of performance parameters for payments, and other recent financial stressors, school/hospital agreements are in disarray on many campuses; as one dean rued: "…we are up to our ears in consultants, lawyers, and dueling documents."

In the majority of schools, funds flow fluctuates from the hospital to the School of Medicine based on a *formulaic calculation* that takes into account paying for services rendered by the faculty to the hospital. The data-driven formula is commonly reviewed by the hospital and school every 3–5 years. To develop a formulaic bottom line split usually requires a several-months-long engagement with a consultant (e.g., ECG) who "unwinds" the fair market value of the contributions of the medical school faculty to the medical center. It is recommended that the expense for a consultation of this nature be borne equally by the medical center and the School of Medicine so that the resulting report will be viewed as fair by both entities.

Any consultation should also include a review of *resident expenses* over and above the total dollars in the cap that the medical school receives for resident support. Of importance, *governmental funds for residency support have continued to wane* over the past decade such that what was once a 60/40 split of costs between the medical center and the school is now in the 80/20 range. As such, if the allocation has not been reviewed within the last 5–10 years, an annual $1 million–$2 million "historical" expense for resident support unfairly falls on the budget of the School of Medicine.

In addition to the well-defined funds flow, it is also recommended to develop an *incentive plan* by which the attainment of specific hospital goals results in additional funds being transferred to the School of Medicine specifically to support education and research. A plan of this nature also facilitates alignment goals. As such, if the hospital's margin, days in cash, or cost per patient hit specified annual targets, these additional hospital profits are shared with the dean's office. Alternatively, it may be as simple as the medical center doing better than budget, with a specific percentage of the overage (e.g., a bottom line split of 3%–10%) coming to the School of Medicine. In this manner, the faculty members are made aware that their endeavors in behalf of the hospital benefit not only the hospital but also the school. These *discretionary dollars*, which can range from $4 million–$12 million, may electively be redistributed by the dean to the school's most productive/deserving departments or used by the dean for programmatic support or recruitments in the basic sciences.

Clinical funds enhancement

Augmenting clinical funds touches on five areas: clinical productivity, revenue cycling, patient access, physician work ethic, and contracting. For the most part, the goal is to *increase profitability* through growth rather than pruning; although both are needed, the former empowers and inspires, whereas the latter creates a sense of unease throughout the organization.

1. **Clinical productivity**: Increasing *clinical productivity* begs the question of your culture. Moving an institution toward a "culture of caring" will increase clinical volume while serving the mission of community service. In this regard, a mandate by the dean for each department chair to create individual faculty charters within a mentorship model can help align clinical work with salary expectations. One can then develop a RVU model whereby salary is based on a fixed dollar amount per work RVU or a salary/bonus plan *based on dollars collected for work done*. Of the two, the latter is more likely to result in a fiscally favorable result. Indeed, it is optimal to reduce fixed salaries as much as possible and work within a system of monthly or quarterly bonus payments based on dollars collected. Also, the expense for benefits is often far less for bonus payments (7% range) than for salary adjustments (30% range). Salary increases can be considered based on the amount of bonus dollars received over a 2-3 year period (e.g. salary increases would be capped at 25% of the average of the total annual bonus over a 2-3 year period). With the bonus intense model, the likelihood of the dean's office being saddled with expenditures for unearned salaries largely vaporizes.

   The individual faculty's productivity needs to be expressed in a tangible manner ("what gets measured gets done"). A *monthly individual report* can take the form of a simple chart tracking all three parameters (charges, collections, work RVUs) on a month-by-month basis within a year-over-year format, allowing each faculty member to compare current with past performance. Further, the *sharing* in each department of deidentified individual performance data may serve as a potent stimulus for less active faculty to work harder. Among the faculty, it should become common knowledge that in order to earn a salary at the 50th percentile of the AAMC, the faculty member needs to be working at the 70th percentile of work RVUs.

2. **Revenue cycling**: Efficient *revenue cycling* (i.e., billing and collection) is key to success. An efficient billing process should decrease billing costs to less than 10%, closer to the community

standard of 8%. Consultation with a firm (e.g., Huron Consulting Group) that will come into your organization and review and revise billing practices will pay the highest dividends in the long run even though the initial dollar outlay may be high. Obviously, the ability to have all departments on one billing plan also reduces costs; however, this is a Catch 22 because any departments that already have an efficient billing system will not entertain throwing their lot in with the general campus until parameters similar to what they have attained are achieved by the larger unit, and yet the economies of scale necessary to drive the costs downward cannot be achieved until all programs join the same billing enterprise. To build trust in the billing and collection process, it is essential that the billing/collections office provide *monthly report cards* with regard to their effectiveness; this report should display monthly statistics for each of the following six areas for each department and center (the industry standard for each parameter should be displayed at the top of each column): billing costs should be < 10%, average days in accounts receivable should be < 55, collections vs. the allowable collectable should be > 95%, charges denied should be < 5%, days from claim received to claim mailed should be < 5 days, and accounts receivable unpaid beyond 90 days should be < 25%.

3. **Access**: It is futile to push clinicians to see more patients, if *community access* to the medical center is difficult. The call center is the point of first contact for most patients, and its efficient functioning is vital to every clinician's practice. Similar to the billing enterprise, performance data from this unit need to be provided monthly to all of the department chairs. There are two paramount metrics that need to be included on this report: % of calls abandoned (industry standard = < 10%) and average speed to answer (industry standard = < 20 seconds). Of note, approximately 40% of abandoned calls occur within the first 10 seconds!

4. **Work ethic**: If effort is expended to optimize both the billing/collections and call center offices, then the quid pro quo is that the *physicians' work ethic* must be similarly in step. In that regard, *standardization of office hours* to 4-hour sessions and *attention to office cancellations* are important. Canceling office hours abruptly creates a major problem, as the fixed costs for running the office have already been incurred, and additional expenses develop as each patient affected by the cancellation needs to be contacted, canceled, and rescheduled. Many patients will elect

to go elsewhere. This type of activity can be rapidly curtailed if the importance of clinical care is hard-wired into the culture along with making income dependent on service provided. *Standardizing a campus-wide policy* with regard to the abrupt cancellation of office hours and proper attention by the department chair goes a long way to curtailing bad behavior (e.g., office hours canceled with less than an 8-week lead time without a reasonable excuse such as illness or death in the family. (Depending upon how "broken" your clinical culture is, this task may fall to the Dean.) Indeed, if office hours are canceled within the 8-week window without an acceptable cause, one may consider the seemingly drastic step of charging the expense of that lost session to the practitioner or to their home department. Similar to work RVUs, it is important to share patient satisfaction reports with each practitioner via a comparison grid such that each faculty member knows where she or he ranks among their deidentified peers.

5. **Contracting**: The true value of the administration to the clinical faculty is realized in the realm of *aggressive contracting*. The hospital and school need to negotiate contracts together such that one is not advantaged to the detriment of the other. This process needs to be transparent and well-communicated to the faculty. The size of the faculty and its expertise often enables the negotiation of a much higher compensation scale than exists in the community. The faculty need to be made aware of this clear benefit of working at an academic health center.

In addition, the respondents provided multiple **tips** with regard to realizing excellence within the clinical mission:

1. **Share**: Identify those departments that have been most successful clinically and visit with the chair to determine the sources of success (e.g., office organization, billing practices, collections, interaction with the call center). Disseminate this information to all chairs.
2. **Volunteer faculty**: Capitalize on your older volunteer faculty to introduce newly hired specialty-specific physicians to community practitioners in order to build their referral base.
3. **Incentive programs**: Mandate that every clinical department must have an *incentive program* that has to be reviewed and approved by the Dean's office. The program should have goals that are RVU based as well as other factors important to the department (e.g., good citizenship as demonstrated by attendance at Grand Rounds, participation in faculty meetings).

4. **No budget/no bonus**: Make it a policy that faculty bonuses cannot be paid unless the department is fiscally solvent. The only possible exceptions to this policy would be pediatrics and family medicine; however, even here, the department needs to be on budget even if that happens to be based on an expected shortfall.

5. **Geographic expansion**: Identify areas that are not well served in the community and open *satellite offices* in those subspecialties (e.g., sports medicine, pain clinic).

6. **International expansion**: This is a more difficult endeavor but can be successful in driving business from abroad to your hospital provided you have the recognized expertise that international patients may be seeking and provided that you are willing to put into place the necessary infrastructure to attract and properly serve patients from abroad.

7. **State agency support**: Consider providing medical services to *state agencies* (e.g., workman's compensation, disability evaluation, prisons). For some of this work in remote areas or in prisons, telemedicine may be employed.

8. **Government reimbursement**: Consult with your CFO to see if the upper payment limit for federal matching funds through Medicaid applies to your state. Deans in Texas, Pennsylvania, and Virginia have realized significant benefit from this program.

9. **Leakage**: It is essential that people insured by your school's health plan are seeing your physicians and not going outside the system. Similarly, your physicians need to refer to their colleagues and to your infrastructure (i.e., radiology, pathology) in order to use your facilities to their full capacity. Your strongest supporters should be the people you employ.

On a more *personal decanal level*, maintaining "boots on the ground" knowledge of the clinical enterprise and engendering the respect of the clinical faculty and medical students can be accomplished simultaneously by *continuing to practice* in one's given area of medical/surgical expertise. This practice, akin to being a "player-coach" or "managing by walking the floor," provides the dean with first-hand knowledge as to the "feel" of the campus; your visibility in the clinical setting convinces people that indeed, you are "in-touch" and you care. However, given all of the other decanal responsibilities, it is not surprising that *only 30% of the deans* were still practicing, and among this group, one-fifth did so only for the first 5–8 years of their tenure as dean and then stopped. Among the few deans still practicing, on average only 10% of the Dean's time was devoted to his/her own clinical work.

While pursued by the minority of deans, *maintaining your clinical skills* provides one with an "out" should the dean's position be a short-lived experience. The value of continuing practice was perhaps best represented by the simple statement: "Tomorrow I may no longer be dean." (Leave no doubt: you are most definitely the President's or the Chancellor's "get out of jail free" card; when a crisis arises, the most common knee-jerk leadership response is to fire the dean.) Also, knowing you have a "clinical or research parachute packed" empowers you to follow your conscience in every circumstance. As one dean stated: "The definition of a spayed administrator is an administrator who is neither willing to be fired or to quit over a matter of principle... (as they) don't know how to make a living other than as administrators."

18. PHILANTHROPY

Blue ocean or crowded seaport? Of all the things you may do as a dean, *philanthropy* will very likely determine your legacy. When you enter the position, you will be introduced to a cadre of community leaders who are very supportive of the medical school. Your job is to keep these individuals engaged while simultaneously expanding the group.

On average, 10%–15% (half a day each week) of a dean's time is spent in philanthropic endeavors. The range, however, is broad, from less than an hour a week to a high of 30 hours/week. This time is spent primarily in attending advancement meetings or one-on-one meetings with high-capacity donors (median of 3 visits/month [range 1–8 visits]).

Suffice it to say that there is no school on your campus with greater daily contact with new and diverse members of the community than the School of Medicine and its associated medical center. Every day, hundreds of people interact with the medical school's faculty in a meaningful manner. Grateful patients, if provided the proper opportunity, will often manifest their gratitude philanthropically; however, "Grateful tears dry quickly." In general, there is a finite period, usually 3 months, during which those who have benefitted from your medical center are willing to be contacted by advancement and are amenable to active involvement with the School of Medicine/medical center. It takes a village of medical school-specific advancement personnel and a lot of time and effort by the dean to maximize this potential resource, which is replenished on a daily basis.

In the beginning, you should visit with the head of advancement for the university to understand his/her philosophy and planned approach to philanthropy specifically, for the School of Medicine. This individual will *make or break your philanthropic efforts*. Sadly, although the strong support of philanthropy in the School of Medicine would seem a no-brainer, at all too many medical schools, it is given short shrift. As one dean noted, "We have a centralized Office of Development. This organizational structure has not worked well for the College of Medicine, and we have often found ourselves in conflict with the development office administration on setting goals and pursuing leads and clients." If this is your situation, you can progress only by either appealing to the President or Chancellor of the University to allow the School of Medicine to have its *own separate advancement effort/team* for which you are willing to pay OR you are going to have to break a few rules in order to advance your school. If you do nothing, you will get nothing. The risk is worth taking.

"By their actions so shall you know them." In an institution where advancement understands and values the School of Medicine, the director/vice chancellor of university advancement should engage the dean of the School of Medicine by introducing him/her to one or more members of the board of trustees who are interested in the university's involvement in health and by creating a meeting between the dean and the person from advancement who has been placed in charge of philanthropy for the School of Medicine or for the health sciences. These are key individuals. The advancement person for the School of Medicine should become part of your inner circle and should be an individual with whom you meet weekly. Also seek the council of the former dean, as he or she will know which individuals in the community are committed to the success of the School of Medicine and the obstacles that need to be overcome; the former dean can also share with you her or his evaluation of the effectiveness of the current advancement team.

The creation of a *Dean's Council* (e.g., Friends of the Medical School Society, Visiting Committee), that has philanthropic and possibly also an advisory/strategic function is also of benefit. In this regard, a medical school-oriented trustee is an invaluable aid in bringing together a strong group of individuals. However, in reality, *only half of the responding deans* have been able to create a council of this nature. For many, this activity has been pushed either up (left within the overall purview of the Board of Trustees) or, more commonly, delegated down (i.e., development of a broad variety of departmental or disease-specific councils: cancer center, heart center, Alzheimer's center, visual sciences center, aging center, diabetes center). The former situation usually is not the choice of the dean but rather mandated by the head of advancement/university central administration; as one dean noted: "The major philanthropic work is tightly controlled by the President of the University. I help when asked, but it is not my primary responsibility."

If you form a Dean's Council, members can contribute in three ways: *time, talent, or treasure.* Some individuals will provide all three, but in the final analysis, your council will need to be balanced among these three abilities. The council should have 10–20 members; the larger number may be more desirable given that these individuals are busy and often encounter emergencies that force their absence from even quarterly meetings. Meetings with fewer than 10 members are rarely productive and discourage those in attendance from continuing. Members should come from various backgrounds: Board of Trustees for the University (at least one or two), alumni (two–four), captains of community industry (two–four), and champions of community health (one or two). If the council is to be more strategic than philanthropic, you may seek additional members from past faculty (one or two), present faculty (one or two), and/or other deans, either active and/or retired.

Should members of the Dean's Council pay *dues*? The vast majority of deans eschewed mandatory dues and instead preferred to ask for an unstipulated and unrestricted annual contribution from the members of the council to support the dean's initiatives. Indeed, only two deans had a policy that mandated payment of dues by all council members. The amount was $5,000 or $15,000; the funds so derived were used to support medical student scholarships.

One unique and highly successful approach to a Dean's Council was to create multiple Dean's Councils with different purposes: Strategic, Philanthropic, Alumni, Innovation (members: alumni in pharma, venture capitalists, individuals in hedge funds, small company entrepreneurs). In this mode, the dean developed scores of individuals close to his/her office. Also, in the same school, multiple subspecialty and disease-oriented department-based advisory/philanthropic councils were encouraged to exist alongside the various dean's councils. All the members of these departmental councils were "embraced" by the Dean, thereby greatly expanding the School of Medicine's philanthropic engine to include more than 350 members. "We set records the last two years for attainment and for cash and for (our) annual fund."

How can you tell if your advancement officer is truly worth his/her salt? There are four essential metrics: (1) how often are they meeting with you (should be *weekly*); (2) are they setting aside 30–60 minutes a week to make phone calls with you to prospective donors; (3) are they creating for you two–four meetings/month (i.e., breakfast, lunch, dinner) with influential or high-capacity individuals in your community; and (4) are they working with your alumni liaison such that each year, you are making several trips to other cities to visit with alumni (especially those who have graduated more than a decade ago) in order to update them on progress and challenges in the School of Medicine. In addition, it is key that your advancement person is situated (i.e., "lives") *within the dean's suite*, not in an off-campus central advancement site. It is not uncommon for blue ribbon individuals to drop by your office with whom it would be important for your advancement officer to meet. In this regard, you as Dean must be

114

uncompromising; quite simply, if the rabbit is too far from the hat, the "magic" never happens.

For successful fundraising, you need first and foremost to *hire a true partner* to lead your development efforts; this individual must be simpatico with your objectives for philanthropy and should report directly to you with only a dotted line to campus advancement. That person can be made an Associate Dean for Development within the School of Medicine, and he/she will then require a team. However, if your advancement personnel are all paid through central development, your ability to motivate them will be compromised, as will your ability to hire a sufficient staff to maximize philanthropy within your school.

The most common and important theme among the respondents to the question of how to build a successful philanthropic arm was to *hire and pay your head of advancement and as many of their team as possible.* Along with a dynamic leader for your advancement effort, you need to hire people into medical advancement who can focus on medical student, faculty, and alumni engagement, events planning, communication (dean's letter, etc.), grateful patients, legacy gifts and to serve as a health facilitator for your major supporters (i.e. smooth the path for them to see specific physicians). In addition, advancement within the School of Medicine needs a well-organized administrative staff, one that never misses a benefactor's birthday or important anniversary, works with your administrative assistant to set-up time each week for donor phone calls while also finding time for face to face donor meetings during the month, and effectively co-ordinates your travel schedule so when you are traveling for whatever reason, an opportunity to visit an alumnus or alumna is created. The threshold for hiring personnel into advancement should be low, as these staff will more than earn their keep within their first two years of employment. At the end of the day, advancement each year should generate a sum of gifts that exceeds its working budget three–five fold. As one dean stressed, the key to success was "A strong development staff, which I increased from 3 to 8, which is still way too small." Indeed, in one School of Medicine alone, the Dean noted there were 80 individuals employed in their fundraising enterprise; these individuals were charged with identifying potential donors nationally and internationally and were then committed to developing meaningful relationships with those individuals while facilitating their relationship with the Dean.

Your other partners in philanthropy need to be several community individuals who share your dreams for the School of Medicine and have *clout within the university.* They can often advocate for you with the President or Chancellor and thus to some degree neutralize a less than favorably disposed Advancement Director. They also, if they are trustees, can *provide you with important information and sage advice.* Heed their counsel. Other individuals who can be of great assistance to you with regard to strengthening philanthropy on your campus include senior clinicians and alumni association leaders.

How can you build a **"culture of philanthropy"** on your campus? First and foremost this is a leadership issue that requires creation of a *learning opportunity*. Specifically, you can either develop an internal course on philanthropy or bring in an organization such as Advancement Resources to do a year-long engagement of quarterly evening sessions to educate your chairs and center directors as well as key senior faculty on the whys, wherefores, importance of "test gifts" and basic mechanisms underlying philanthropy. (One dean noted, that by the third session, one of the physicians had worked with an advancement officer to make a successful presentation to a grateful family; together they secured a $250,000 gift for research – this far exceeded the cost of the course.) You can also create campus town halls on philanthropy as all members of your organization (i.e. faculty, residents, students, nurses, ancillary personnel, etc.) should be aware of the importance and impact of philanthropy on the healthcare goals of the organization and the realization that rather than asking individuals for money they are offering grateful patients and their family an opportunity to "pay it forward" that will benefit future patients and their families. As one dean related, it was impressive to have trustees and donors talk to an auditorium packed with physicians, nurses, medical assistants, etc. on the power of philanthropy and why they elected to provide support for a given need in the medical center. Lastly, in fostering a culture of philanthropy it is very important to "celebrate" philanthropy as it occurs. Philanthropic gifts should be highlighted in the dean's electronic newsletter and should be posted widely on campus through all forms of communication that are at the disposal of the dean's office. Philanthropy should also be part of any discussion by the dean regarding progress within the School of Medicine. Philanthropy will only be woven into your culture if YOU are pulling the thread.

Additional decanal advice regarding philanthropy included the following:

1. **Alumni: Medical Students**: This is often an underutilized resource. You may need 2 or 3 advancement personnel to minister specifically to this group. Development of 20, 25, 30, 40, and 50 year reunions on campus and year specific fundraising campaigns can be very beneficial especially with regard to raising scholarship funding. Also the older alumni are an important group with respect to developing legacy gifts. A separate *legacy gift officer* on your

advancement team is a worthwhile expenditure as he/she can interact with patients as well as senior alumni.

2. **Alumni: Resident/Fellow**: Each department should expend some effort to connect with their specialty specific residents and fellows. Invitations to resident graduation, discounts for on- campus specialty courses, notices about departmental visiting professorships, and receipt of a departmental quarterly or biannual newsletter are all *"touches"* that may translate into philanthropic support. As with medical students, this group of individuals is also a prime point of contact for your legacy gift officer.

3. **Alumni: Faculty**: Both prior and emeritus faculty members can provide funding for various important projects. Invitations to major school events and receipt of the dean's newsletter are helpful in this regard. Again, these individuals may also provide legacy gifts.

4. **Strategic Plan**: Philanthropy should be a prominent area of focus in the strategic plan. Fundraising objectives need to be clearly defined – both in purpose and amount (e.g. student scholarships, curriculum support, seed money for research, endowed chairs, new buildings, etc.).

5. **Dean's travel**: Consider having your advancement person review your travel schedule for the year with your administrative assistant. Visits can then be created to alumni in that particular city. As one dean noted: "regularly meet alumni where I am scheduled to go for meetings." You have graduates all over the country; to not visit with them when you are in a city for whatever other reason is a missed opportunity. Alternatively, purposely set up a couple of trips a year to a few major cities in which the largest number of your alumni reside.

6. **Dean's Healthcare Facilitator**: This person may be your administrative assistant, your deputy chief of staff, or a specific nurse/physician. This person is responsible for ministering to the healthcare needs of trustees, donors, dignitaries and their family and friends; the facilitator is on "speed-dial" for these individuals serving as a knowledgeable liaison with the clinical faculty.

7. **Gala**: Galas are a lot of work and cost; however, they are major friend raising events while also generating a minimum of six figures and commonly a million or more dollars for the school. This is where trustees can introduce their campus naïve friends to the School of Medicine. Also, your medical students are phenomenal ambassadors for the School of Medicine; assigning a medical student to every table to facilitate the attendees' enjoyment of the evening is a worthwhile endeavor. Nobody is more passionate about your School of Medicine and the importance of a medical education than the students. The Gala is also when every department chair can invite a handful of her/his grateful patients to participate; the chairperson should know that the department will receive a portion of the proceeds from tables occupied by their faculty and community supporters.

8. **Be prepared**: What is your *elevator speech* when someone says to you: "What do you need?" As Dean, you should always have at front of mind a *logarithmic list of asks* based on your assessment of a donor's capacity should he/she inquire: "What would you do if I could provide you with (____ fill in the blank - $10,000, $100,000, $1,000,000, $10,000,000, $100,000,000+)?" Respective thoughts in ascending order could be a one-time invited lecture or seed funding for medical student summer research experience, medical student tuition relief for two students, endowment of a fellowship or funding of a specific research endeavor, creation of multiple endowed chairs or naming a department or a building, or the pinnacle goal, naming the School of Medicine.

9. **Listen well**: Does the person with whom you are speaking have an expressed passion for a particular area within the School of Medicine or the general campus? If so, even if it is not in your personal vision, encourage the discussion. *Don't ever try to steer a donor away from their passion*; it is fine if the outcome supports a project that was not on your radar screen or even if it results in funds going to another school in your university – this good "deed" will (may) eventually come back to you.

(*Caveat: Advancement Philosophy: the prevailing philosophy in advancement is to find one or several individuals of high net worth ($1 billion or more), curry their favor over years of relationship building, and convince them to give millions to the institution. There is little stomach for "crowd-sourced" fundraising from less "able" grateful patients; however, the latter can also be a source of substantial funds given the number of contacts each physician has on a monthly basis. The downside for "crowd-sourced" fundraising is the amount of effort that needs to be put into place to raise sums of $100,000 or less; still small "test" gifts can grow to larger size and one should never underestimate the potential gift of a seemingly "small" capacity donor. While the single donor – million dollar approach is understandable, the appeal to the "crowd" is not without merit and indeed the author has now seen chairs come to fruition based on a seed gift followed by literally 100's of smaller contributions from individuals who had benefitted from their relationship with a given faculty.)

19. THE ACADEMIC SENATE AND THE GOVERNING BOARD (WHO'S PULLING YOUR CHAIN?)

"The ultimate achievement is to defeat the enemy without even coming to battle."
—Sun Tzu "The Art of War"

As one responding dean advised: "You have all the power in the world, until you go to use it." To be sure, you will encounter various and sundry members of your own faculty senate or council who will *bedevil you*, either wittingly or unwittingly, as they seek to enhance their own standing by opposing the Dean. Indeed, you will be mystified at the number of individuals who in the spirit of "shared governance" will invariably push forward their own agenda or simply oppose any measure you wish to initiate unless it benefits them directly. Even more disappointing is that these self-serving souls will not take responsibility for their actions and will invariably claim that everything they did was to benefit the School of Medicine.

As such it is important for you to choose your friends wisely and your enemies more wisely; *in the halls of the ivory tower, friends come and go, enemies accumulate.* As such, it is helpful for you to seek out your most successful chairs and your most trusted faculty and encourage them to become active members of the senate and of the senate's executive board. ("The solution to pollution is dilution.") The more individuals who are actively engaged in the Senate who have an appreciation and commitment to the new culture and the school's new strategic plan, the better.

For many schools of medicine, the academic senate exists only for the general campus and the participation of the medical school is limited to a couple of representatives. In this situation, there is often a faculty council that serves as a liaison for the dean. In other cases, rather than a faculty council there is truly a separate senate for the School of Medicine with its own executive committee and President. In either case, it is in the best interests of your School of Medicine and your ability to function effectively to get to know each of the key individuals. As one dean lamented: "I meet with the Senate executive committee or the Senate assembly when invited. I have not set up regular visits which was likely shortsighted on my part."

Communication, collaboration and transparency are the paths to creating a senate/council/board experience that is empowering and positive. The following suggestions are a compilation of the responding deans' suggestions:

a.   Meet monthly with the President of the Senate or the Chair of the Faculty Council or the executive committee of the faculty council or the assembled School of Medicine senate; during this time outline your upcoming report to the senate or council (vide infra: d) and work with this individual/committee to develop the agenda for upcoming Senate or Council meetings. Over half of the deans at a school with either a Faculty Council or School of Medicine Senate recommended the monthly meeting format.

b.   Attend all School of Medicine senate or Faculty Council meetings. Again more than half of the Deans with either body recommended attending the monthly meeting.

c.   Consider attending the campus-wide Senate meetings at least twice a year and offer to provide an update on the School of Medicine.

d.   Quarterly, at the senate or faculty council meeting provide a report on the School of Medicine's progress in the clinical, administrative, research, teaching, service (i.e. community, legislative, and philanthropic areas), and financial realms. Also this is a perfect time to vet new policies and ask for advice.

e.   If you report directly to a **Board of Trustees or Board of Directors** it is important for you, if possible, to attend all of their meetings, meet with the leaders of the Board's committees that impact the School of Medicine (e.g. Finance committee), ask for an annual opportunity to present an update on the School of Medicine (if this is not already required), and befriend members of the Board who are particularly drawn to the School of Medicine. (Caveat: If you are going to meet with a trustee or board member and you are planning to discuss philanthropy for the School of Medicine, for the sake of transparency you should clear this first with your university's Chancellor or President or Associate Vice Chancellor for Advancement.)

20. CRISIS

Crisis prevention is preferable to crisis management. The best you can do is to be ever vigilant and proactive. Seek out the molehills and attend to them immediately. In this regard, one dean noted that at his/her school, there are biweekly meetings convened by the Chancellor's office to review any crises or potentially negative impactful situations in addition to a monthly meeting with legal counsel to review all major campus legal matters.

What are the six steps that can be taken to cap a crisis when it occurs?

1. **"Is everyone safe?"**: Fortunately most crises are not ones that entail physical harm, but if this is the case activate the *emergency response system and notify campus police.*

2. **Take a breath and proceed to assess the crisis**: As one dean noted your first move is to: "…take your own pulse." Next, calmly map out the crisis as to its *type* {research, clinical, public, educational, personal (faculty, staff, student), legal, practice plan, natural disaster, discrimination, sexual harassment}, *scope* {intrauniversity, community, regional, state, or national (federal)} and *risks* to the university (public image, legal, and financial). At this stage, all communication should be either "in person" or "by phone" (*nothing in emails, twitter, etc.*). To be sure, a face to face meeting (or a personal phone call – distant second best) with the individuals who are directly impacted by the crisis is important. Seek information from each of the primary players *individually*; during these interviews and always have a third person in the room to take accurate notes. Get the facts while they are *fresh*. Take the

time to "work the problem NOT the people involved." Resist the temptation to knee-jerk fire/chastise those involved, you need to obtain all of the facts before acting at a personal level. Root cause analysis and personnel actions come later.

3. **Create a plan**: Once the problem is defined and you have completed the necessary interviews, then take 10-30 minutes, to create a *list of things to do and proceed to prioritize them*. Next review the potential plan with your most trusted "second in command" and then with legal counsel.

4. **Notify your direct superior**: Inform the President or the Chancellor about the crisis, your analysis (vide supra – step 2) and potential remedy (vide supra – step 3) (both for responding to the crisis and for communications/public relations). As one respondent noted: "I have a low threshold for informing the chancellor of bad events, but this is more for informational than for intervention(al) (purposes)." By the same token, if you are coming to the chancellor with a crisis, you had better come prepared with at least *one or two feasible solutions*. The chancellor needs to see that you have expended quite a bit of time and energy to rapidly define the crisis, interview the involved players, and develop a reasonable plan of action.

5. **Assemble your "crisis" team and assign tasks**: This team will be responsible for developing the *communication plan* (both internally and externally), *strategy*, and *tactical objectives*. A *spokesperson* needs to be appointed and the press should be allowed to only speak to that one individual. No other persons on your team or at the university should speak to the press, but rather refer them to the spokesperson; this needs to be communicated to all stakeholders in the first communication about the crisis. So who is "on the team"? As one dean answered in a "no-duh" fashion, "The crisis team depends upon the crisis." However, there are a few *players that are commonly involved* in all crisis situations: legal counsel, communications lead, and your most trusted second in command (e.g. vice dean, senior associate dean). A list of others that you may consider depending upon the nature of the crisis include: senior deans, human resources, selected chairs, VP of facilities, VP of research, VP of education, security/campus police, public relations, associate dean for faculty affairs, head of IT, environmental health and safety officer, and/or student president. *For clinical concerns* the following individuals may be asked to serve on the crisis committee: hospital CEO, CFO, CMO, VP of faculty practice,

hospital president, director of risk management, compliance officer, CSO, director of marketing, President of Faculty Practice Plan, President of Medical Staff, and/or Hospital board chair. Lastly, in rare cases, the University EVC/Provost may be on the team if they so desire but for the most part they will receive rather than help create your report since the EVC/Provost is commonly responsible for final decisions and thus needs to remain shielded albeit informed by you of developments as they progress. The leadership needs to be able to trust that they will hear what they need to know from you rather than learn about the situation from others. You need their *TRUST*, but don't be surprised or "take it personally" if they go around you and do some of their own fact finding and damage control; that is just the nature of university politics especially when their position may also be on the line.

6. **Communicate**: Notify ALL key individuals_well before there are any items in the press or on the air waves. As one dean noted, "I did always rather be accused of over communicating rather than under communicating." This includes *stakeholders* with regard to the particular crisis as well as key people who support the university such as donors or political figures and the chair of the board as well as the hospital's CEO (after all you are partners in this endeavor). The initial communication might be an emergency meeting *limited* to the members of the affected department or institute or a meeting with all of the chairs and directors again depending upon the nature of the crisis. The next step is a more general communication which may take the form of an "email broadcast", texts, a campus wide page alert, announcement on the campus intranet followed by a community meeting, faculty meeting, or student meeting as befits the situation. You may also consider providing *a webcast* to the entire campus community and to select key individuals (donors, local politicians, etc.). In some universities, this is made quite easy as there is an emergency system that once activated sends a message out by text, voice mail and email simultaneously. Lastly, if indeed the problem is at the federal level, you may want to alert your congressional delegation. You should have a low threshold for going to Washington, meeting with the appropriate agency individuals, acknowledging the error/problem and discussing how it is being addressed and remedied.

Table 3: Checklist for handling a "crisis"

Immediate Actions (Day one)		
	a.	Decide if there is a need to activate *emergency response system* (yes/no)
	b.	Define the *type of crisis* (research, clinical, educational, personnel, natural disaster, financial)
	c.	Assess the potential *scope of the crisis* (intrauniversity, community, regional, national)
	d.	Determine the *risk* to the university (public image, financial, legal)
	e.	*Limit communication* to in-person or phone
	f.	*Interview primary "suspects"* individually (with a third person in the room to take notes)
	g.	*Create a plan* (to do list / prioritize) (with second in command + legal counsel)
	h.	Notify your *direct superior* (share your plan of action / desired spokesperson / potential crisis team members)
	i.	Appoint ONE *spokesperson*
	j.	Assemble *crisis team* to further "flesh" out plan of action (communication, strategy, objectives)
	k.	*Communicate* (stakeholders – university and community) (Get out in front of the story and stay there!)
Subsequent actions		
	a.	*Root cause analysis*
	b.	*Personnel actions*

Finally, what is the *timeline* for taking these six steps? Key here is that as soon as you learn of the crisis, you need to *document your immediate response* as you now "own" it. The first four steps (vide supra) should, in most cases, be completed within the day – *don't let the sun set* on the crisis as you need to get your information "fresh" (i.e. before those involved have an opportunity to talk to each other and begin to possibly alter their story) and develop your plan expeditiously, as well as communicate the foregoing with your direct superior. You need to be both in the moment and in the "future" as everything you do in response will be subject to later scrutiny and your timeliness in that regard will play a prominent role in how you are judged.

21. EVALUATION: YOU! AND YOUR TEAM

*The biscornette, a gargoyle that sits on an upper balustrade of the cathedral of
Notre Dame symbolizing to all below
"the perils that beset talent cultivated in vanity unaccompanied by humility"*

You. To whom do you report and how do they assess your performance? If you are not being assessed, are you then truly valued? In just over 80% of cases, an *annual decanal report* was part of the evaluation process; however, in only a quarter of the cases, was a self-evaluation (i.e. leadership abilities and personal accomplishments) part of the submitted report. The report/*self-evaluation* preceded an annual meeting with the Chancellor, President, or Chair of the Board of Directors to review progress made toward previously set goals and to develop goals/metrics for the coming year. Rarely, every 3-5 years the Board requests an external review of the dean (one case) or the dean is reviewed via an internal faculty survey.

Interestingly, 20% of the deans noted they had no formal annual report required or face-to-face annual review. Some noted an annual conversation with the Chancellor/President while others noted that this occurred sporadically, was superficial, and devoid of substantive feedback. In several cases this lack of review could be attributed to the fact that medical school deans and chancellors/presidents seem to enter and leave the university by the same whirling revolving door with a complete revolution occurring every 2-3 years. Without feedback, can meaningful progress occur? Or as one dean opined: "If you aren't catching flak, you aren't over the target."

What of the *personal leadership development* of the dean? Two thirds of the deans had undergone a *360°evaluation.* This exercise is lengthy and at times painful as it may bring into conflict your self-image with how you are actually perceived by colleagues, co-workers, and subordinates. Not surprisingly, several deans felt this analysis was not to be taken seriously: "My opinion is that the comments are anonymous and can be disheartening. I would rather have the president make an evaluation and then inform me where he thinks I can improve." As another dean surmised: "Since I am still in office after 16 years, my evaluations must be satisfactory."

Indeed, *accepting the 360 degree* evaluation is akin to three of the phases of going through the diagnosis of a life-threatening illness: *denial* ("I feel I have enough high level support that I do not need any professional coaching."), *anger* ("The comments were either positive (90%) or negative (10%). I could have predicted the negatives and who wrote them as I have heard it before."), and finally *acceptance* ("Yes, desire to enhance leadership and management skills."). In truth, the perception of your faculty and staff is reality and does need to be addressed. A large dollop of humility goes a long way (vide supra: biscornette) toward enabling one to begin or continue the journey to improved leadership. Without a consensus constituency, you may think you are leading, when indeed nobody is following.

Executive Coaching

Executive coaching was part of the leadership experience for one-third of the deans. The consensus was mixed as to the benefit of this experience. However one dean noted: "A *first rate executive coach*, with business experience has only one goal and that is to make you a better, more successful leader. For a given problem, this person often has a solution to consider that was foreign to you. Being a dean is a "lonely" position – each person in the organization from whom you seek advice is a stakeholder and thus has their own inherent conflicts of interest. Your executive coach is unique in that regard." The operative words here are "first rate". Among executive coaching organizations, on a national basis, Blessing and White is well known and highly rated; however, on many major university campuses there is likely a business school that can provide an effective executive coach at a reasonable expense.

Evaluating Your Team

How do you best evaluate your direct reports? One dean noted performing an annual review of each person on the leadership team specific to their area of expertise. Each person on the leadership team was required to provide an annual report to the dean with regard to progress towards previously agreed upon goals, challenges, and proposed goals for the coming year. With this approach, each aspect of the strategic plan (i.e. clinical, administrative, research, teaching, service to the community, philanthropy, faculty affairs and finance) could be reviewed in depth. By having these meetings several months in advance of the dean's meeting with the President/Chancellor, the information obtained from the leadership group could be used to identify challenges and develop corrective strategies/tactics as well as strengthen the dean's report.

22. LIFE BALANCE

"Life balance is not readily achievable given the demands of the job and if your spouse or partner isn't committed to what you're doing, stress occurs. The support at the home front is needed."

Balancing an all-consuming job with a family can tax even the most organized individual with the most understanding family. So how do successful deans strike a *life balance* that allows them to continue in the position and not lose their family in the process?

For sanity sake and to preserve your family unit, you *MUST take your vacation* time but indeed, for some this was not a wholly attainable goal. As one dean replied: "there are no vacations".

Who minds the store while you are gone? For most deans, when they are out they will have their Vice Dean, Executive Vice Dean or a Senior Associate Dean be the point of contact with assistance from their Chief of Staff; that individual can, as appropriate, delegate matters to the Associate Deans based on their area of responsibility (e.g. research, education, clinical, finance). Signature authority for common things, such as grants, is given to the appropriate senior associate dean but other matters are usually held until the Dean returns. It is key for the designated point of contact to know that while you are away, to the full extent possible you must be informed of anything they see as potentially important (i.e. "no surprises" when you return).

Most of the deans had their *administrative assistant "triage"* their email and forward urgent matters to the appropriate Vice Deans or rarely, despite being on vacation, to them directly. This underscores the importance of having an *outstanding assistant*; in this regard, NEVER compromise as the pain of a poor assistant is exquisite and your loss of face due to their lack of excellence is irreversible. Your assistant must be smart, committed, and proactive in your behalf at all times.

You are out of the office, but *is the office out of you?* Likely not completely. On average, most deans would call "in" 1-2 times per day and check their email at least once a day in order to preclude a mountain of email when they returned. Still the time spent on email work and phone calls was in general severely limited and often done early in the morning or late at night when "the rest of the family is otherwise preoccupied". One dean, for trips abroad of 1-2 weeks duration, set up a separate temporary Gmail account known only to his assistant and a few higher ups. Only triaged key emails were forwarded to the new, temporary account by the dean's administrative assistant.

While the consensus was to check-in once or twice daily, there were a minority of deans at either extreme. Some deans noted that even on vacation they were "always available, 24/7" ("I handle vacation time poorly."); one dean noted that they believed that their "open door policy" throughout the year "may lead individuals to bug me less when I am on holiday." There were only two deans who totally "unplugged" for days or a week by traveling to a remote wilderness site where phone contact and internet access were absent. They put on their out of office message and clearly designated an individual to handle everything. (A suggestion: If you are confident or brave enough to do this, then consider returning from vacation on a Saturday so you have an entire Sunday to clean out your email and get back to the present rather than dealing with stale email and issues for several days after your return while new issues are piling up; this eliminates the nightmare of reentry which can rapidly terminate any resurrection of spirit and body that might have occurred while you were away.)

How much time should one take for vacation? For many deans, a couple of vacation days are tacked onto an out of town meeting either on the front or the back end. For others it is "catch as catch can" and amounts to only a few days. However, for other deans, an annual 1-2 week vacation is planned; this is often done 6-9 months in advance. As one dean noted, this is "a good move!" Frankly, your ability to walk away from the office for at least a week is an indication of your confidence in your staff and a manifestation that you believe you have done the job sufficiently well that: a.) you have earned this time off and b.) the place can continue to run well in your absence (for at least a week*). You are only indispensable to your family, never to your job.* Not a single dean replied that they needed to take LESS vacation.

So how do you *balance work and family?* The overwhelming majority of deans appeared to be chained to their digital device ("The cell phone and email are never off." "I am always available." "I am never inaccessible. It is never the case that I do not look at my email or take phone calls or turn my cell phone off." "I am always connected." "I know, it's a pathology, but a common one.") And yet, despite this ongoing almost all encompassing digital commitment, several deans clearly voiced their commitment to family ("I do make family and my personal life a priority." "Nothing is more important to me than my family." "From the very start of my career…I made an absolute commitment that my family would always take precedence over my work. There are days on end, perhaps even weeks on end, when the casual observer might feel that I was abandoning this commitment…"). One wonders who is fooling whom, as even the youngest member of the family can distinguish the difference between word and action.

Preserving family time when you are on the job would seem to be of great importance and yet only 2 deans did so with any absolute regularity. For one dean it was the concept of honoring the Sabbath with the family – no emails, no meetings, no phone calls allowed. For another dean it was particularly important to "shut it down" evenings and weekends not necessarily because of the family but rather to preserve the strength and sanity of the staff. : "I *do not* routinely read work email in the evenings or on weekends between the time I leave Friday evening and Sunday afternoon. I found that if I do, it means my staff (must) read their email and respond to my email, resulting in a vicious chain of everyone working on what are generally routine things. This is not fair to my staff."

A compromise position for several deans was to make sure that the family knew before the week began what nights they would definitely be home for dinner, in other words, *what hours truly belonged to the family* (i.e. the email and phone are shut down or put on stand-by), and what part of the weekend was set aside for family time. As one dean noted: "I have a very understanding wife and do periodic checks of email at specific times on weekends and vacations. This allows me to only spend 20-30 minutes to "check in" and see if there is anything requiring my response." Another dean noted: "I do not carry my cell phone when I am with my grandchildren." Indeed, several deans did draw a line on the weekend. Some would declare a part of the weekend email and cell phone free (e.g. Saturday at 3PM until Sunday noon – time for a date and to peruse the Sunday New York Times). These carved out periods need to be fully honored – *the world will wait, your family won't*. Was it worth it?

How much *weight* is literally brought to bear on the dean at a *personal level*? First, with all of the donor dinners and other events it is not surprising that one third of the deans found themselves gaining anywhere from 10-15 pounds. ("The amount of consumable food in this job far exceeds my ability to say "no" to it." "…started when I turned 40 of gaining about one pound a year despite my best efforts to show reasonable restraint in my diet. *I am absolutely convinced this reflects an increase in the gravitational pull of the earth.*"). Half of the deans maintained their weight while around 15% noted a 5-10 pound loss of weight. Among all the replies, there was one classic decanal response (i.e. an answer meant to satisfy the questioner while offering neither commitment nor information): "I never weigh myself. I focus on eating and exercising for health, not on a specific weight target."

To *maintain health* just over 2/3rds of the deans exercise regularly (3-7 days/wk.): gym membership, elliptical machines, running, cycling, swimming, home gym, etc. A few deans have a personal trainer scheduled to come to their home a couple of times a week for an hour session, usually very early in the morning. Other activities include walking (22%), golf (14%), skiing (6%), and sailing (6%). Other *one-off* activities included: tennis, yoga, opera, tai chi, photography, gardening, stamp collecting, classical music, reading, and cooking. There were no marathoners or triathletes in the group. Others placed a high priority on eating right (11%) and on sleeping well (6%).

How many deans partake of that over which they preside? Only one third of the deans noted they had an annual medical examination. ("Now have a physician but ignored this for many years."). One dean noted, that it is always difficult to find new physicians for your family when you move and suggested finding out from your predecessor the physician(s) who provide(d) care for him/her and their family. These are usually the very best physicians on the campus. But like the cobbler's barefoot children, the majority of medical school deans fail to visit with a physician on an annual basis.

23. POST LOG: MOVING ON: TIMING

"Do not end your career on the bench."
(Jim Brown retired from the Cleveland Browns in the year
he was named the Most Valuable Player in the National Football League!)

Knowing *when to step down* is one of the most difficult aspects of the dean's position, presuming you are provided that opportunity (as one Dean noted: "You either call your own shot or you get shot."). Indeed, several deans (14%) noted that they aspire to leave at the top. However, defining the "top" may be difficult. For some, a *specific objective* goal needs to be attained (e.g. fiscal solvency, child finishing high school) or *time in the saddle* attained (e.g. completion of a 10 year term). In contrast, for others the goal is far more elusive: "when the medical center is in the best situation to adapt for the future of healthcare, research and education." At the opposite end of the spectrum, is the decision to leave based on *failure*: health, evaluations, or lack of accomplishments; indeed, this was the criterion for just over 1/3rd of the respondents. In between these two extremes is *what the majority of deans replied* (57%) that the decision to step down was more of a *gestalt* than an event or a date: "...an evolution than an epiphany", "not fun anymore", "...see all of the obstacles and few of the opportunities.", the daily routine becomes "overwhelmingly irritating", "do not feel like going to work." or when "...your optimism has curdled". As one dean surmised: "When I wake up in the morning and no longer have a sense of purpose, motivation, and excitement, mixed together with a tinge of anxiety and fear, it will be time to step down."

In this regard, the *annual review*, if you have one, and most certainly, your *term review*, at 4-5 years, are excellent opportunities for you to step back, reflect on the past, assess the present, and then proactively decide whether to stay or to go. If you find yourself answering the question with a question: "What will I do if I don't do this?" or "How will I make ends meet if I don't earn this salary?"…then you have already answered the question – and now is more than likely the time to move on. In reviewing the nearly forty answers to this question, it became clear that several deans were already struggling with their future: "I know that my energy and stamina are not now what they were …when I began this journey." "I am getting tired of some of this."

There is one other circumstance to which you need to be alert and that is the sound of the "gun being cocked". Specifically this occurs when a new President of the University or new Chancellor is appointed. Given the amount of funds the Vice Chancellor/Dean of the School of Medicine controls (often 50% or more of the entire university), it is not uncommon for the new President to seek to hire his/her own Vice Chancellor/Dean of the School of Medicine. When the President or Chancellor who hired you announces their departure, this is a very good time to take stock of your position and possibly call your own "shot".

Once you make the *decision to retire* from being dean, the next step is to decide the *timing* of your formal announcement. Initially your decision is shared with your President, Chancellor or the like in confidence and together you can decide when to make the formal announcement. Once that decision is discussed and the announcement is made however, you are now a "lame" duck and your ability to expend resources becomes more circumscribed as the leadership will want to preserve as many resources as possible to attract your successor regardless of the fact that you may have "earned" those resources. Many deans feel that a *9-12 month lead time* is appropriate as it should give ample time for the Chancellor or President to perform a search and identify your successor and if all proceeds expeditiously, possibly provide for a 1-2 month overlap so the new dean can work with you to better understand the idiosyncrasies of the institution and its faculty. Anything briefer, unless an internal "heir apparent" is available, will create an inter-regnum period that at best maintains the status quo and at worst initiates a downward slide. Also you need to disabuse yourself of the notion that you will have the opportunity to either groom or select your successor; that is most definitely the exception, not the rule.

What is the *exit strategy*? First and foremost, when you leave, *LEAVE!* Do not fall into the bitter trap of second guessing your successor and commenting on his/her progress or lack thereof. As one dean noted: "I will do my best until the day I leave, but what happens after that, I really can't or will not try and control."

Fully one fourth of the deans begin their post-dean time with a *SABBATICAL.* This step-down sabbatical should be part of your initial hiring package. With or without a sabbatical, the overwhelming most common postdecanal path (42%) is to return to clinical practice, either full or part time. Other paths cited by the remaining one-quarter of the deans included working on a corporate board, working as a special project coordinator for the university, returning to the laboratory, consulting, creative writing, or seeking another position either in industry or as a Chancellor or Vice President of Health Affairs. Only 20% of the deans planned to retire completely.

Final Musings

Being Dean of a School of Medicine is a tremendous opportunity to do much "good". It is an exhilarating and all-consuming activity. Timing is key with regard to how long to stay and deciding when to stop. Your plan for leaving should be well thought out before you begin, for only then will you always be able to act decisively and 100% in accordance with your principles throughout your span in the dean's office. In the final analysis all races, end – only in this one the length of the track is in flux.

Appendix I: Questionnaire

General:

I. What preparations did you make for this job? Did you take a course and was it useful?

II. What was the biggest surprise you encountered in the Deans Office (i.e. for what were you least prepared)?

III. During your tenure, have you had any epiphanies with regard to your role as Dean (i.e. moments in which a revelation occurred that inalterably changed your approach to a given area/challenge)?

IV. What do you view as your greatest success and what factors allowed for that to occur? Was there a special moment or tactic that created a turning point in realizing the goal?

V. Looking back, was there a decision that you wish you could take back or reverse? What were the factors that led you into making that decision and knowing what you know now, how would you have done things differently?

VI. If you could describe yourself in one word, what would that word be?

The following are a series of questions that relate to the broad range of decanal activities. Feel free to dictate/write answers to as many of them as you see fit; it is fine to send answers in a very rough form. Unless otherwise indicated by you, no names will be associated with any given answers, anecdotes, or suggestions. For the education questions (i.e. 10 a-g), given their detailed nature, please feel free to involve your Senior Associate Dean for Education.

1. In the beginning…Organization and infrastructure:
   a. Knowing what you know now, what would be the first and foremost piece of <u>practical</u> (i.e. actionable) advice to your successor?
   b. In your Vice Chancellor/Dean's office do you have any <u>positions</u> that you consider **unique**? If so, what is the title and the purpose of that particular position and how important is it in your organization on a scale of 1-5 with 5 being vital?
   c. Do you have a Vice Dean? If so what is his/her primary role? What is their value to your organization on a scale of 1-5 with 5 being vital?
   d. When you are on vacation, to whom, if anyone, do you delegate decanal authority?

2. Hiring and Negotiation
   a. How do you comprise your search committees: specifically who is the typical chair of the search committee and what

categories of people do you have on the search committee (e.g. senate member, members from the given department, people from associated hospitals, psychologist?).

b. What are your instructions to the search committee (e.g. confidentiality – sign/not sign a statement; number of candidate visits; recommend how many candidates for the position from which the dean will select one?)

c. When a chair position becomes vacant, is there anything "special" or "unique" that you do to identify potential candidates beyond the usual advertising in the various journals and posting on the university's website?

d. When do you involve a search firm? How do you select one?

e. Do you have a favorite means of negotiation with a new chair to determine the size of the offer package?

f. Do you perform a "reverse site visit" when evaluating the final candidate for a chair position? If yes, what "new" information are you seeking?

g. Do you differentiate a temporary chair by using the terms "interim" (i.e. placeholder) vs. "acting" (i.e. potential chair candidate)?

3. Mission, Vision, and Goals: Formulating a Strategic Plan

a. How did you go about developing a strategic plan for your school? How long did it take? Did you involve an outside agency (if so, whom) and how would you rate that agency on a scale of 1 to 5 (best)?

b. How did you implement your strategic plan?

c. How often do you review progress on your strategic plan?

d. At what time point do you plan to do a major revisit and overhaul of your strategic plan?

4. Culture change

a. How do you define your culture?

b. How do you reinforce your culture?

5. Branding and marketing

a. Have you undergone a branding exercise for your school? If so, what firm did you use? What was the cost and how satisfied were you with the outcome on a scale of 1 to 5 with 5 being excellent?

b. What metrics have you used to assess the impact of your branding/marketing exercise (i.e. increased applicants to your school, improved applicant pool, etc.)?

6. Faculty/Chairs development

a. Are you expending resources to further develop the leadership abilities of your chairs? If so, what are the specific actions you are taking (e.g. leadership courses, finance courses, executive coaching, etc.)?

    b.   Do you have a specific set of metrics for annually evaluating the performance of your chairs? If yes, please include a copy of that evaluation grid with your other answers.

    c.   Do you employ any methods to either incentivize or reward your best Chairs/departments? If yes, what are they?

7.   Communication

    a.   What is your policy with regard to having cell phones, laptops, tablets at meetings (e.g. eFree meetings, laptops only, etc.)?

    b.   How often do you meet with your "boss" (e.g. the Chancellor or Provost)?

    c.   How often do you meet with your chairs one on one? How long are these meetings? How are they structured?

    d.   Do you have any regular occurring meetings that you consider to be relatively **unique** (e.g. quarterly town hall meetings, state of the school annual address, etc.)? If so, what are they and what is their specific purpose?

    e.   Do you have any secrets for managing email?

    f.   Are you on Facebook, LinkedIn, Twitter? If so, how often do you post information on those accounts? Who monitors these accounts for you or do you do this yourself on a daily/weekly basis?

    g.   Do you "text"? If so, how much time each day does this involve?

    h.   Do you use "voicemail" on your personal/cell phone?

8.   Solvency: the cost of freedom

    a.   What is the biggest cost saving endeavor that you have undertaken and how much was saved?

    b.   What is the biggest "blue ocean" (i.e. new source of funding) that you have identified? How was it implemented and how much new funding did it realize?

    c.   Do you have a Dean's Discretionary Fund? If so, how much funding is there in that account ANNUALLY for you to use as you see fit to grow/develop the School of Medicine?

    d.   Does your school have a formula that provides incentives to faculty?

9.   Research: sustainability

    a.   Are there any new/unique research programs that you have begun that have been particularly beneficial?

    b.   In days of waning federal support for research, what has proven to be the biggest source of alternative research dollars for your university? How did you initiate or enhance this endeavor?

c. Have you maintained any part of your own research program and grants?

d. How does your school handle indirect funds from research grants?

e. Do you receive a portion of clinical revenue for school operations and is this determined by a formula?

10. Education: maintaining credentialing

a. Given the fiscal challenges to support education, have you begun any new/unique programs to provide for <u>additional funding</u>?

b. Aside from match day and White Coat, are there other ways in which you interact/engage your students on a personal level (e.g. student lunches, happy hours, student dinners, social clubs, etc.)?

c. Do you have any specific exercises or practices that you have found to be particularly beneficial in helping prepare you for the LCME visit?

d. What kind of curriculum do you have (departmental based / organ based / system based, etc.)? Do you anticipate changing it, and if so to what?

e. What are your thoughts on the use of digital technology, simulation, and flipped classrooms as part of the medical education process?

f. How much of your required curriculum is devoted to medical ethics? In what year of training do these classes occur?

g. How much, if any, of your required curriculum is devoted to medical humanities? In what year of training do these classes occur?

11. Clinical challenges

a. What measures have been most successful at your institution in achieving clinical alignment/integration with the medical center?

b. How have you worked out a viable funds flow model between the School and the Medical Center? Do you have an institutional incentive plan (i.e. a process whereby if the hospital is doing well, then there is a formulaic funds flow to the school to support education and research) in place and if so, how does this work?

c. What have you found most helpful in the quest to further enhance clinical revenue (e.g. culture change, improvements in revenue cycling, development of new clinical programs based on consultant research)?

    d. Are **you** personally still practicing and if so what percent of your time is involved? If yes, what is the reason you elected to continue to work clinically?

12. Philanthropy

    a. Advisory council: Do you have a lay/community advisory council? If so, how many members are on it? What is its stated purpose (e.g. strategic, philanthropic, etc.)? Does each member make an annual donation to be on your advisory council? If so, is the amount specified and how much is it?

    b. What per cent of your time each week is devoted to philanthropy? On average how many **one on one** meetings/meals with potential donors do you have each month?

    c. What or who has been your greatest aid in your philanthropic efforts?

13. Senate / Board of Directors

How have you developed integration with either the Senate or your Board of Directors (e.g. monthly meetings with the Senate executive committee, a dean's office senate liaison, etc.)?

14. Retention

    a. At what point do you initiate efforts with a faculty with regard to offering a retention package (i.e. when a faculty member states they are looking, states they have been invited to interview, has been to a place for one visit, has made a second visit, states they are on the "short list", has an offer letter in hand)?

    b. If you do a retention agreement, are there any steps you take with regard to precluding the need for another retention exercise with that individual over a specified time period (e.g. have the faculty sign as part of the agreement that they will not seek another retention endeavor for a specific period of time)?

15. Termination/Firing

    a. What are the key events that might lead you to ask a Chair to step down (e.g. lack of solvency, poor clinical performance, faculty revolt, etc.)?

    b. Whose counsel, if any, do you seek in this regard (e.g. your cabinet, other chairs, provost/chancellor, hospital CEO, etc.)?

    c. Are there any intermediary steps with regard to rehabilitation/salvage that you may take prior to finalizing the action (e.g. anger management course, leadership course, executive coach, etc.)?

16. Crisis
    a. What are your first steps when first informed of a crisis (i.e. legal counsel, provost/EVC, etc.)?
    b. Who is on your "crisis" team?
    c. What steps do you take to communicate with faculty and staff?

17. Self-evaluation
    a. Have **you** personally undergone a 360 degree evaluation? If so, what prompted this action?
    b. Have **you** personally engaged an executive coach during your tenure? If so, what prompted this action?
    c. How are **you** evaluated annually? (Are you required to complete your own performance evaluation with stated goals, progress, and a leadership self-evaluation? Do you have an annual review with your provost/chancellor or board of directors?)

18. Life Balance
    a. How do you handle your vacation time? (e.g. do you designate your email to someone else? Is it truly "down" time? Is there ever a time when you make known that you are inaccessible?)
    b. How do you balance your family time (e.g. specific times during the week/weekend that are **solely** for family – during which time you are not looking at your email or taking phone calls, cell phone turned off)?
    c. How do you maintain your own health and well-being? (e.g. physical trainer, exercise time, walking meetings, meditation, yoga, annual medical exam, etc.)
    d. How much weight have you gained/lost since becoming Dean?

19. Moving on
    a. When will you know that it is time to step down?
    b. What is your exit strategy (i.e. return to practice, career change, sabbatical, retirement, etc.)?

(Author's note: The numbers next to the major topics on the questionnaire do not line up with the numbers of the book chapters as these were rearranged as the book was constructed in order to provide for a more logical flow of the text.)

Appendix II: Request form for the dean to speak at an event

Request for the Dean's Attendance at an Event

Speech Information Request Form

DUE 14 DAYS BEFORE EVENT

ABOUT THIS REQUEST: Thank you for the timely and accurate completion of this form, which will ensure that Dean _____ delivers the best possible speech at your event.

DIRECTIONS: Please take some time to fill in the spaces below, providing as much information and including as much detail as possible. Boxes will expand as you type... **Please email the completed form to - _____, at _____ (email address) before _____ (date 14 days prior to the event). Please call _____ (dean's office number) if you have any questions.**

Requesting Organization/Department (Name):

_____

Speech Contact Person:

Phone #:

Email Address:

	Event Name: Date: Time: Location:
Event Details	

	• What is the purpose of the event? • Why are you having the event? Why now?
Purpose	

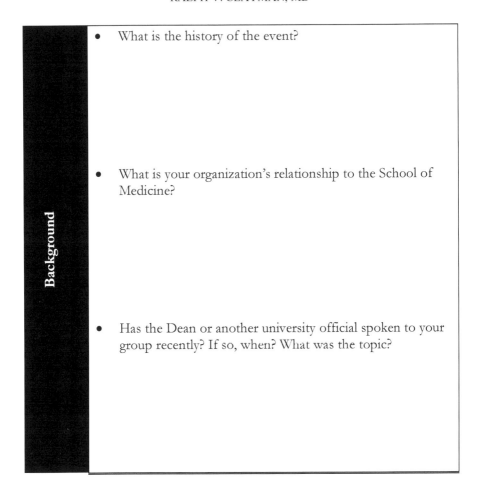

Background

- What is the history of the event?

- What is your organization's relationship to the School of Medicine?

- Has the Dean or another university official spoken to your group recently? If so, when? What was the topic?

Audience

- Who will be attending the event? Please include a proportional breakdown of the audience by categories, such as 50 percent students, 25 percent parents, etc.

- How many people will be in the audience? Please attach a guest list if available.

- What are the key messages to be communicated?

- Please list specific points or examples that the Dean can use to support these key messages. Please provide detail in the points below.
    1.
    2.
    3.
    4.
    5.

- What do you think the audience wants to hear?

Messages

- Are there any issues or concerns of which the Dean should be aware?

Logistics

- How will the event unfold? What is the setting?

- Will the speech be an introduction, standard remarks or keynote address? If intro, who is the Dean introducing and please attach that person's curriculum vitae and bio sketch?

- Length in minutes:

- Any special video/audio components?

- Will media be attending?

- Will a photographer be present and can the Dean have access to the pictures?

- Will there be a Q&A with the audience?
    If so, how long (minutes)

Program

- Who will provide the Dean's introduction? What does the Dean need to say about this person?
  (Please include that person's curriculum vitae and bio sketch.)

- Does the Dean need to acknowledge or thank any individuals or groups?

- Who else is speaking at this event? If possible, attach agenda or schedule.

- Will the Dean need to introduce anyone following him on the program? (If so, then please attach that person's curriculum vitae and bio sketch.)

Other Concerns

- Is there anything else we should know to help ensure the success of your event?

Appendix III: Enculturation Schedule (new faculty orientation): Two day schedule

<u>DAY ONE</u>

8:00 am-12:00 pm	Department Orientation: Department Administrator
12:00 pm-1:00 pm	LUNCH
1:00 pm-1:30 pm	Welcome: Chief Executive Officer
1:30 pm-2:15 pm	Medical Staff Orientation: Chief Medical Officer
2:15 pm-3:00 pm	University Physicians and Surgeons: Senior Associate Dean for Clinical Affairs / CEO, University Physicians and Surgeons
3:00 pm-3:15 pm	BREAK
3:15 pm-4:00 pm	Quality and Safety: Associate Dean for Clinical Operations
4:00 pm-5:00 pm	Tour of the Medical Center

<u>DAY TWO</u>

7:30 am-8:00 am	Continental Breakfast
8:00 am-8:45 am	Welcome: Mission, Vision, Values: Dean
8:45 am-9:30 am	Academic Affairs: How to Get Promoted: Executive Vice Dean and Associate Dean for Academic Affairs
9:30 am-10:00 am	Faculty Development: Associate Dean for Faculty Development
10:00 am-10:15 am	BREAK
10:15 am-11:00 am	Faculty Compensation Plan: Director, Compensation Plan
11:00 am-12:00 pm	Walking Tour of medical school campus
12:00 pm-1:00 pm	LUNCH

1:00 pm-1:15 pm	Research: Overview of Opportunities: Senior Associate Dean for Research and Graduate Studies
1:15 pm-2:00 pm	Research Administration: Contract and Grants Manager
2:00 pm-2:45 pm	Compliance: Staying out of Trouble: Assistant Dean - Compliance
2:45 pm-3:15 pm	BREAK
3:15 pm-4:00 pm	Medical Education: Senior Associate Dean, Medical Education
4:00 pm-4:45 pm	Graduate Education: Associate Dean, Graduate Studies
5:00 pm-6:30 pm	Dean's Social

Appendix IV: Sample Theme and supporting Goal and Strategies plus metrics

UC Irvine Health – FY14 Q3 Strategic Plan Progress Report
Theme – Advance Premier Research

Goal 4 – Develop disease-focused multidisciplinary and translational research.

Strategy 4.1: Foster greater research collaboration between faculty at the School of Medicine and the main campus

Metrics		FY13 Baseline	FY14 Target	FY14 Q1 – Q3	FY15
1	Collaborative publication and abstract accepted at national symposium, 1 in FY14 and 2 in FY15.	2 abstracts	1 publication	0 publications	
2	Grant application to extramural funding agencies stemming from the Seed grants and collaborations, 1 in FY14 and 2 in FY15.	In progress	1 application	2 applications	

FY14 Q3 Activities / Accomplishments:
- Received and reviewed 6-month reports from 3 active projects; all appeared to be making good progress meeting milestones set at activation meeting. One project (Detection of single bacteria in blood infection in minutes, Dr Zhao PI) already resulted in the submission of a DARPA grant.
- Re-engineered Strategy 4.1 plans for coming year, adding to the "topic driven" pilot grants a Career development grant component modeled on NIH K-series grants, and a clinical coordinator initiative, aimed at providing a structured organization of clinical research coordinators across multiple projects (including coordinator training for certification).

FY14 Q4 Planned Activities:
- Continue ongoing interaction with PIs of active projects for mid-term reports, monitoring progress, identifying possible obstacles and providing guidance for successful conclusion
- Planning or Q3 year-end dinner for currently active projects, to be held at the University Club in the summer 2014; during the dinner awardees will present results from completed projects, in conjunction with presentations from other awardees from parallel programs (i.e. Dean's triumvirate awards)
- A meeting of this strategies' champions will be scheduled to discuss and plan next year topics for new call for applications; if the increase in funding that was requested at the stage of planning for the next year will be approved, the general plan will be to increase the total number of funded projects to 4-6, divided into two topic areas as opposed to the single focus area utilized in the prior issues of the award.

FY14 Q4 Anticipated Challenges:
- No major challenges are expected for the coming quarter

Strategy 4.2: Strengthen translational research that builds upon strong basic science and enhances collaboration between basic and clinical researchers.

Metrics		FY13 Baseline	FY14 Target	Q1	Q2	Q3	Q4
1	Peer reviewed funding obtained by members who have received a Triumvirate Grant or Biumvirate Grant. $800,000 or more in both FY14 and FY15.	$4.18M	$800,000 or more	In Progress	In Progress	In Progress	
2	Peer reviewed grant submissions by members who have received a Triumvirate Grant or Biumvirate Grant. 1 new grant submission in both FY14 and FY15.	N/A	1 new grant submission	In Progress	In Progress	32 new submissions	
3	Collaborative peer review research grant funding by attendees at Dean's Dinners. $500,000 in both FY14 and FY15.	$404,429	$500,000	In Progress	In Progress	In Progress	
4	Publications by 2 or more individuals as co-authors who attended a Dean's Dinner. 3 publications for each FY14 and FY15.	3	3	In Progress	In Progress	In Progress	

FY14 Q3 Activities / Accomplishments:
- All three campus-wide Topic Directed Dinners scheduled: Vision 3/18, Speech 4/3 and Movement 5/14.
- Vision topic directed dinner completed.

FY14 Q4 Planned Activities:
- School of Social Ecology (SOSE) and SOM Brainstorming Dinner on 4/28
- SOSE and SOM Turnaround dinner hosted by the SOSE, date TBD
- Topic directed dinners: Speech 4/3 and Movement 5/14

FY14 Q4 Anticipated Challenges:
- N/A

*(N.B.: The **tactics** to support the strategy included: 1.) Triumvirate grants: creating a grant that required 3 principal investigators: one from a clinical department, one from a research department in the School of Medicine, and one from a school other than the School of Medicine 2.) Biumvirate grant: grant with a principle investigator coming from the School of

Medicine and from the Veterans Administration hospital, and 3.) Dean's Dinners: 25 invitees from the School of Medicine and 25 invitees from another school on campus (e.g. arts, engineering, biological sciences, humanities, etc.) on a first come first serve basis – there was one dinner at the hospital and a turnaround dinner at the other school's facility on the main campus)

{Funding: For fiscal year 2013, a total of $327,000 was dedicated to the theme for Advance Premier Research of which up to $185,000 was earmarked for Goal 4.2: – triumvirate grant ($75,000 – $50,000 for the top grant submitted and then up to two $15,000 grants for the two runner-ups if deemed to be of sufficient quality), two biumvirate grants ($50,000 each), and the interschool dinners ($10,000 budget).}

Appendix V: Consultants for Strategic Planning

- AMC Strategies LLC: carmichaeld@amcstrategies.com (Los Angeles) (888) 406-7086
- AltshulerStaats LLC: (Brookline, MA) jill@altshulerstaats.com 617.879.1750
- ECG Management Consultants: (facilitator): Clay Tellers ctellers@ecgmc.com (San Diego, CA) 858.436.3220
- Noblis: – Falls Church, VA (offices in Baltimore, Washington DC, San Antonio, and West Virginia) 703.610.2000 http://www.noblis.org/solutions/Missions/health
- TRUE POINT (Boston, MA) graham@trupointadvisors.com
- http://trupointadvisors.com/business-consulting 303.520.6607

Appendix VI: Strategic Plan: Four Point Meeting Schedule
(Acknowledgment to Steve Cesca: University of California, Irvine)

- 1. August: All hands on deck 2 hour meeting: Strategic Plan Steering Committee, School of Medicine and hospital leadership, and all strategy co-champions come together to review the end of fiscal year report and quarter 4 (i.e. the annual) progress for each of the strategies.
- 2. October: All hands on deck 1 day retreat: Strategic Plan Steering Committee, School of Medicine and hospital leadership, and all strategy co-champions. The plan is reviewed and priorities for the coming academic year are similarly reviewed. Strategies achieved or no longer feasible are retired and new strategies and associated tactics are developed. (N.B.: Quarter one reports from the strategy

co-champions are due in November and are reviewed without a meeting by the leadership – problem areas are identified and those co-champions may meet individually with leadership to discuss the challenges in their area.)

- 3. February: Strategy specific focused 20-30 minute meetings: School of Medicine and hospital leadership, and *strategy specific* co-champions. At this meeting quarter 2 results are reviewed for each individual strategy and the co-champions' draft proposal for tactics and *funding requests for the coming year* for their strategy are reviewed. (This may require *upwards of 10 hours* of time from the leadership over the month of February including a separate one hour meeting of the School of Medicine and hospital leadership to *approve* funding for each strategy for the coming year.) (N.B.: Approved funding for the various tactics proposed is then communicated to the strategy specific co-champions. Additional meetings with the strategy co-champions would occur on an ad hoc basis should there be questions/concerns regarding funding or tactics.)
- 4. May: All hands on deck 2 hour meeting: Strategic Plan Steering Committee, School of Medicine and hospital leadership and strategy co-champions meet to review quarter 3 progress and to review the strategies/tactics/funding approved for the coming fiscal year.

(For members of the strategic plan steering committee the annual time commitment is one day plus 4 hours (2 – 2 hour meetings). For the strategy co-champions, they have an additional formal meeting in February and possibly a follow-up meeting if they are not meeting their targets. For the executive leadership they are committed to the 2, two hour meetings, the one day retreat, and an additional 10 hours of meetings with strategy co-champions.)

Appendix VII: Charging the Search Committee

Dean's Charge to the Search Committee:

1. Definition: This is a search committee whose job it is to find and filter applicants for the position and then forward to the Dean 2-3 names in alphabetical order of recommended candidates so a selection for the position can be made.

2. Overview of the Department.

   a. Last internal review of department by campus (chair's review – redacted)

   b. Last state of the department document

   c. Fiscal review

   d. Dean to provide 3 key outcomes for the new Chair to achieve in their first 3 years.

3. Skill set and competencies to do the job:

   a. Committee needs to develop the standards or indicators for the level of PERFORMANCE to be a leader

   b. Committee needs to determine the BEHAVIOR necessary to meet the institution's demands

   c. Do NOT rely just on weight of CV or research $$$.

   d. Request a cover letter of each person submitting a CV. The cover letter should be one or two pages at most and include a statement about the candidates' qualifications, skill set, leadership philosophy, values, approach, and vision for the department.

4. Culture: basic assumptions about the world shared by a group of people that determine their perceptions, feelings, and behavior

   a. Culture of clinical/translational research: discovery

   b. Culture of education: teach

c. Culture of caring: treating patients like family using the most advanced and innovative forms of diagnostic testing and therapies: heal

d. Culture of philanthropy: generating and promoting community support – concept of our need to be "value added" to the community

e. Importance of diversity and equal opportunity. Please ask the Associate Dean for Faculty Affairs to attend one of your upcoming meetings to review this key part of the search process.

f. This is an opportunity to show off our campus

5. Committee members

a. You were selected because each of you represents different areas of the institution which the successful candidate should be able to address – education, research, clinical care, and administrative abilities – both infrastructure and fiscal.

b. It is your job now to think from an institutional standpoint such that the successful candidate will not only be able to minister to the needs of the department but will also integrate well into the overall campus and be value added to the institution – horizontal integration is key.

c. I will ask of each of you to be candid, diplomatic, have forbearance, discuss and disagree without ever becoming disagreeable, and most of all to put the needs of SOM first and foremost.

d. Would you like to include any of the following: medical students, nurses, residents, administrators, or community leaders on the search committee?

e. Key: recruit the FAMILY.

6. Confidentiality: essential

a. Sign the confidentiality statement

b. Respect for the candidate and for the process

    c.   Any questions regarding the search should be deflected to the Chair of the Committee

    d.   Note that we have members from the Department on the Committee and thus we are entrusting you with the greatest commitment to confidentiality and integrity as members of the department will try to obtain information about the search from you. The ability of the process to work rests on the integrity of each individual of the committee.

    e.   No search committee member should contact other individuals with regard to a candidate unless specifically instructed to do so by the Chair of the Search Committee.

    f.   <u>Confidentiality is PERMANENT</u>. At no time present or in the future should the disclosure of the activities of the committee be made to anyone. Failure to maintain confidentiality will result in immediate dismissal from the committee and preclude future service.

7.   Administrative assistance: (recruitment coordinators)

    a.   Dean's office: Executive Assistant and Administrative Assistant

    b.   Associate Dean for Administration and Finance

    c.   Each candidate is assigned an "administrative navigator" who will be with them each time they visit and facilitate their flights, hotel arrangements. Etc. This person will also evaluate the candidate.

8.   Interview process

    a.   First visit: two days

    b.   Second visit: with wife/family

    c.   Phone interviews (need to be uniform in questions asked – inform the candidate that this is planned and seek their approval)

9.   Timetable for when a short list should be available to the Dean

10. Closure

    a.   If they have not been selected as a candidate to interview— needs to be a letter signed by the Chair of the Committee.

    b.   When after they have interviewed they have not been selected to continue in the interview process needs to be a letter from the Chair of the Committee to the candidate.

    c.   Reliance on the committee members to help with successful integration of the newly chosen chair into the campus community.

    d.   Ground work with departmental members with regard to the new Chair for acceptance of that individual

11. Dean's role: I am here to help you help us. I am more than happy to call references, etc. at the request of the Chair of the Committee.

Appendix VIII: Phone Questions of Candidate's References/Contacts

Name of person contacted:

Title and place of work:

Relationship to the candidate (supervisor / peer / mentee):

How long has this person known the candidate?

When was this person's last contact with the candidate?

Is this person currently working with the candidate?

1. How long and how well have you known Dr. X?

2. Do you believe Dr. X has the energy, interpersonal skills, leadership, and administrative talent to lead a department?

3. What kind of decision maker is Dr. X?

4. How would you characterize Dr. X's leadership style?

5. What are Dr. X's greatest strengths?

6. What are Dr. X's greatest weaknesses?

7. With respect to leading and managing a department, where do you think Dr. X will have the most difficulty?

8. Have you ever seen Dr. X manage a serious conflict in faculty or staff? How was his/her performance?

9. What would you say Dr. X's main achievement has been at xxx University?

10. Do you believe Dr. X has the desire and fortitude to engineer positive change in a challenging academic environment?

11. If you were Dean, knowing what you know, would you hire Dr. X to be the Chair of a busy and challenging department of _____?

Appendix IX: Chair Competencies

Evaluation of competencies/how this chair achieves results.

Leadership – Promotes high standards in the areas of teaching, research and service; communicates priorities and administrative procedures effectively; articulates a vision for the future; demonstrates listening skills; provides national and statewide visibility and recognition for the department and university; through committee work and other endeavors, contributes to the leadership of School and University.

Administration and Management – Oversees the recruitment of highly qualified faculty, staff and leaners; provides support for successful recruitment and retention; manages the department effectively and in a fiscally responsible manner; seeks input on and accepts responsibility for decisions; provides effective budget management; makes decisions in a timely manner; is proactive in assessing strengths and weaknesses of the department; able to respond to potential problems early thereby preventing their escalation to crisis status;

Diversity – Encourages diversity; implements mechanisms for attracting and retaining underrepresented groups; responsive to culture, ethnic and gender diversity; demonstrates and encourages respect for all persons in the department and across the University.

Collaboration – Practices sound techniques of collaboration, openness and shares governance, and encourages others to do so. Fosters an environment of teamwork and collaboration.

Planning – Works effectively with faculty, staff and learners to identify appropriate goals, set priorities, and focus resources in the department and across the university. Has developed and implemented a strategic plan.

Development – Works to identify and pursue philanthropic support for the department; develops support for the University at all levels – public and private.

Personnel Development – Provides guidance, support and resources for faculty and staff development, particularly in promotion, tenure, and evaluation; demonstrates impeccable judgement and fairness in each academic action; provides succession planning.

Assessment – Effectively, accurately and objectively evaluates the department and its components, acknowledging areas of excellence and recommending improvement where needed.

Academic Freedom – Supports and defends academic freedom as it is relevant to the department.

Education – Supports and fosters a climate that promotes excellence in teaching.

Research/Creative Activity – Supports and fosters a climate that promotes excellence in research/creative activity.

Collegiality – Actively works to create an environment where faculty, staff, learners, and visitors feel welcomed, appreciated, and heard.

Patient Care – Where appropriate, supports and fosters a climate that promotes uncompromising excellence in patient care.

Appendix X: Metrics

(For each metric there can be a goal and a stretch goal that will allow for ongoing assessment of performance during the year – these can be placed on a spreadsheet along with a column for a quarterly or mid-year assessment of progress)

Metrics: CARTS (Clinical, Administrative, Research, Teaching, Service) plus finances

Clinical:

Total work RVU:

Work RVU/full time faculty member:

Department average for 1st available and 3rd available appointment:

Ambulatory patient volume (e.g. 5% growth):

New patients seen in the ambulatory environment (e.g. 5% growth):

Inpatient volume by hospital admissions (e.g. 5% growth):

{For surgical department: total number of inpatient operations (e.g. 5% growth)}

{For surgical department: total number of outpatient operations (e.g. 5% growth)}

Length of stay improvement (e.g. decrease by x percent):

Decrease in readmission rate (i.e. 3%) or other "national initiative":

Progress on a "hospital-based" initiative (e.g. % of patients discharged before noon):

CMS composite score (e.g. 99%):

HCAPS score (individual areas each with a goal/stretch goal) (e.g. communications with physicians/pain control/etc.):

Press-Ganey scores (e.g. improvement goals):

Administrative:

Departmental diversity:

Complete renovations in a particular area

Complete business plan for expansion (e.g. new office site /new line of business)

Faculty retention rate:

Faculty expansion (new hires):

Publish a state of the department annual report:

Publish a quality and safety annual report:

Percent faculty eligible for promotion who got promoted:

Implementation of a mentoring program:

Residency accreditation:

Collaborative endeavors with other departments/schools:

Research:

NIH Funding:

Indirects realized:

Total research funds for fiscal year:

New grants received:

    a. peer reviewed

    b. industry

    c. philanthropy

Grants submitted:

    NIH:

    Other peer reviewed:

    Industry:

# of podium sessions at annual national meeting:

# of posters presented at annual national meeting:

# of publications (peer reviewed) by the department:

Cumulative impact factor of all peer-reviewed publications for the year:

# of book chapters written by the faculty during the year:

Dollars of funding per square foot of research space:

Education:

4th yr. student evaluation of clinical clerkship:

Medical student performance on that discipline's national shelf exam:

% of 4th year medical students seeking a residency in the given specialty:

Timeliness of grade submission:

ACGME survey reports on the residency program (i.e. accreditation without citations):

Number of applicants per residency program position:

% residency match with medical students from top tier medical schools:

Resident performance on national boards (% passing on first attempt):

National courses held by the department:

Fellowship accreditation:

Local/regional courses held by the department:

Faculty receiving national teaching award:

Faculty receiving School of Medicine teaching award:

Service:

a. Philanthropy

Endowed chairs:

Philanthropic dollars realized:

Philanthropic dollars pledged (i.e. </= 5 years to realization):

Philanthropic dollars pledged (i.e. > 5 years to realization):

b. Community

Outreach programs to schools:

Interaction with community groups:

Free clinics sponsored by the department:

Finances:

Profit/loss statement:

Departmental carryforward:

Performance based on prior year budget (over, below, or on budget by what % - goal $\pm$ 10%):

Conversion to a new financial plan (e.g. RVU compensation plan):

Miscellaneous: Professional development of the individual chair:

Leadership courses taken:

Executive coaching endeavor:

360 degree evaluation completed:

Appendix XI: Chair Incentive Plan: example for the Chair of Medicine

US News and World Report Best Hospitals Rating in any of the areas below: Cancer, Diabetes & Endocrinology, Gastroenterology, Heart & Heart Surgery, Kidney Disorders, Pulmonology, Rheumatology	Departmental Imputed Work RVUs	NIH Funding For Medicine Departments	Teaching (National Courses held on campus) (School-wide or national teaching awards for faculty)
Top 50*	60th percentile*	Top 50*	1 course or award*
Top 30*	70th percentile**	Top 30**	2 courses or awards**
Top 20***	80th percentile***	Top 20***	3 courses or awards***
Top 15****	90th percentile****	Top 15****	4 courses or awards****

Achievement of any of the parameters would result in a Z bonus each year in which they occurred up to a maximum of $160,000 in any given year. This would be in effect during the initial 5 years.
* $15,000 for each accomplishment
** $20,000 for each accomplishment
*** $30,000 for each accomplishment
**** $40,000 for each accomplishment

Appendix XII: Medical Humanities Curriculum

Medical Humanities

The First Two Years

The courses in the medical humanities for the first two years have the following goals:

- To become sensitive to and to review some central moral, philosophical and social issue in medicine and health policy.
- To reflect on physicians' traditions and responsibilities in developing and implementing healthcare delivery.
- To develop critical skills for evaluating the moral and philosophical claims, arguments and goals frequently found in medicine.
- To formulate, present and defend a particular position on a moral issue in healthcare.
- To reflect on the relationship between moral, professional and legal obligations of physicians.

The first year course has 22.5 contact hours; the second year course has 24 contact hours. Topics include professionalism, ethics code and oaths, paternalism, informed consent, competency, truthfulness, confidentiality, abortion, maternal- fetus issues, treatment for incompetent patients, end of life decisions, death and dying, physician assisted suicide, research on human subjects, objectivity and bias in medical research, animal research, genetic testing, managed care, healthcare reform, social justice and healthcare, organ donation and procurement, healthcare regulation, ethics committees and medical futility. Grading in these courses is based on exams, class participation and short papers.

The Last Two Years

The topics introduced in the first two years are further discussed in small groups for one or two sessions of two hours each during the third year, as part of the regular pediatrics, internal medicine, obstetrics/gynecology, surgery and family medicine clerkships. The third-year courses provide 8- 10 contact hours through a team teaching approach with clinical faculty and students identifying the issues for discussion (e.g. death and dying, uncooperative patients, unfair aspects of "the system," pain control, and "hot" topics).

The fourth-year medical students have the opportunity to take a variety of month-long selectives in the medical humanities (e.g. History of Medicine, Literature and Medicine, Law and Medicine, War and Medicine, Death and

Dying, Elective in Medical Ethics and Humanities (independent Projects) and Osler, The Man and His Writings). Enrollment has ranged from one third to two thirds of the senior class. There is also a three-hour classroom required portion of the fourth year curriculum for medical humanities.

(Acknowledgments: Dr. Edward C. Halperin, former Dean of the University of Louisville School of Medicine and presently Chief Executive Officer and Chancellor for Health Affairs of New York Medical College and Provost for Biomedical Affairs at Touro College and University System, for the suggestion of the book's title)

CONTRIBUTORS

Philip O. Alderson, MD
Dean, School of Medicine
Vice President, Medical Affairs
St. Louis University

Robert J. Alpern, MD
Dean and Ensign Professor
Yale School of Medicine, Yale University

M. Dewayne Andrews, MD
Vice President for Health Affairs
Executive Dean, College of Medicine
University of Oklahoma Health Sciences Center, Oklahoma City, OK

Karen Antman, MD
Provost, Boston University Medical Campus
Dean, School of Medicine
Boston University

William F. Bina, III, MD, MPH
Dean
Mercer University School of Medicine

David Brenner, MD
Vice Chancellor, UC San Diego Health Sciences
Dean, School of Medicine
University of California, San Diego

Michael E. Cain, MD
Vice President for Health Sciences and

Dean, Jacobs School of Medicine and Biomedical Sciences
University at Buffalo

Paul R. G. Cunningham, MD, FACS
Dean and Senior Associate Vice Chancellor for Medical Affairs
The Brody School of Medicine at East Carolina University

Thomas A. Deutsch, MD
Provost
Rush University, Chicago

J. Kevin Dorsey, MD, PhD
Dean Emeritus
Southern Illinois University School of Medicine

Betty M. Drees, MD, FACP, FACE
Professor of Medicine and Dean Emerita
Department of Internal Medicine and Department of Biomedical and
Health Informatics
University of Missouri-Kansas City School of Medicine

Terence R. Flotte, MD
Dean, Provost, Executive Deputy Chancellor
University of Massachusetts Medical School

John P. Fogarty, MD
Dean
Florida State University College of Medicine

Robert N. Golden, MD
Robert Turell Professor in Medical Leadership
Dean, School of Medicine and Public Health
Vice Chancellor for Medical Affairs
University of Wisconsin-Madison

Robert I. Grossman, MD
The Saul J. Farber Dean and Chief Executive Officer
New York University Langone Medical Center

Roger Hadley, MD
Dean, Loma Linda School of Medicine
Executive Vice President for Medical Affairs, Loma Linda University
Health

Edward Halperin, MD, MA
Chancellor/CEO
New York Medical College

Richard V. Homan, MD
President and Provost, Dean of the School of Medicine
Eastern Virginia Medical School

J. Larry Jameson, MD, PhD
EVP, University of Pennsylvania for the Health System
Dean, Raymond and Ruth Perelman School of Medicine
University of Pennsylvania

Cynda Ann Johnson, MD, MBA
President and Founding Dean
Virginia Tech Carilion School of Medicine

Richard D. Krugman, MD
Distinguished Professor
University of Colorado School of Medicine
Kempe Center for the Prevention and Treatment of Child Abuse and
Neglect

Arthur S. Levine, MD
Senior Vice Chancellor for the Health Sciences
John and Gertrude Petersen Dean, School of Medicine
Professor of Medicine and Molecular Genetics
University of Pittsburgh

Steve Nelson, MD, CM, FCCP
Dean of LSUHSC (Louisiana State University Health Sciences Center)
School of Medicine
John H. Seabury Professor of Medicine
Professor of Physiology

Mark A. Richardson, MD, MScB, MBA
Dean, School of Medicine
President and Board Chair, OHSU Faculty Practice Plan
Oregon Health & Science University

Jose Ginel Rodriguez, MD, FAAP
President and Dean of Medicine
Universidad Central del Caribe School of Medicine, Bayamon, Puerto Rico

William L. Roper, MD
Dean and CEO UNC School of Medicine and UNC Health Care
The University of North Carolina at Chapel Hill

Paul B. Roth, MD, MS
Chancellor for Health Sciences
CEO, University of New Mexico Health System
Dean, University of New Mexico School of Medicine

Arthur J. Ross, III, MD, MBA
Dean & Professor of Surgery and Pediatrics
West Virginia University School of Medicine

Steven Scheinman, MD
President and Dean
Professor of Medicine
The Commonwealth Medical College

David Stern, MD
Executive Dean and Vice-Chancellor for Clinical Affairs
University of Tennessee College of Medicine
University of Tennessee Health Sciences Center

Jerome Strauss III, MD, PhD
Dean, Virginia Commonwealth University School of Medicine
Luigi Mastroianni, Jr. Professor of Obstetrics and Gynecology

Samuel J. Strada, PhD
Dean
University of South Alabama
College of Medicine

James O. Woolliscroft, MD
Lyle C. Roll Professor of Medicine and Dean
University of Michigan Medical School

Anonymous: 2

INDEX

ABOUT THE AUTHOR

Dr. Ralph V. Clayman is a graduate of Grinnell College and the University of California, San Diego, School of Medicine. Following his residency in Urology at the University of Minnesota and an AUA research scholarship at the University of Texas, Southwestern, he spent 17 years at Washington University in St. Louis, attaining the rank of Professor of Urology and Radiology. In January 2002, he became Chair of the newly formed Department of Urology at the University of California, Irvine; within four years, the department was among the top 20 programs in the country. In 2009, he accepted the role of Dean of the UC Irvine School of Medicine. During his five year term as dean, the school of medicine attained full accreditation from the LCME, achieved a positive financial balance, opened over 750,000 square feet of new space, and experienced significant growth in its academic profile. Dr. Clayman is a co-founder of the Endourology Society and is co-editor of the *Journal of Endourology*. He holds 13 medical device patents and has published over 400 peer reviewed manuscripts. Presently he holds an endowed professorship in the UC Irvine Department of Urology. He has a clinical focus on urolithiasis and co-directs the endourology research laboratory and fellowship program.

Made in the USA
Middletown, DE
07 October 2020